Managing Millennials

Managing Millennials

Alan Chelak

2018

DO WHAT THE FUCK YOU WANT TO LICENSE

Everyone is permitted to copy and distribute verbatim or modified
copies of this document, and changing it is allowed as long as the
name is changed.

DO WHAT THE FUCK YOU WANT TO LICENSE

TERMS AND CONDITIONS FOR COPYING, DISTRIBUTION AND
MODIFICATION

0. You just DO WHAT THE FUCK YOU WANT TO.

ISBN: 978-1-387-63703-4

Image 34

compudida.com

Contents

B

The #

The 1 Minute Manager's # B a 1 minute readout from the 😃 of a modern digital 👁 B is intended to remind each of us to take a minute out of our day to 👁 into the 😃 of the 👫 📖 manage. And to realize that 📖 ☞ our most important resources.

B

Introduction

In this brief story, 📖 🎁 😊 with a 🏴 deal of

😺 📖 📙 learned from our studies in 🌱 and in

the behavioral 🐘 about how 🚶 🏢 best with

other 🚶 .

By "best", 📖 😊 how 🚶 produce valuable results,

and feel 👍 about themselves, the organization and the

other 🚶 with whom 📖 🏢 .

This allegory, The 1️⃣ Minute 👤 , is a simple

compilation of 😊 many wise 🚶 📙 taught us and

😺 📖 📙 learned ourselves. 📖 recognize the

importance of these sources of wisdom. 📖 also realize

that the 🚶 who 🏢 with 😊 as their 👤 will

👁 to 😊 as 1️⃣ of their sources of wisdom.

📖 trust, therefore, that 😊 will take the practical

📘 😊 gain from this 🦪 and use it in your

daily management. For as the ⬛ sage, Confucius,

advises each of us: "The essence of 📘 is, 📙

it, to use it".

🎁 🙏 😊 enjoy 🏴 😵 😃 🎓 from The 1️⃣ Minute 🧗 and that, as a result, 😃 and the 👫 😃 💼 with will enjoy healthier, happier and ➕ productive lives.

The 🔍

ONCE there was a bright young 🧑 who was 👁 for an effective 🧍.

🧍 wanted to 💼 for 1️⃣. 🧍 wanted to become 1️⃣.

🤚 🔍 had taken him over many years to the far corners of the 🌍.

🧍 had been in small towns and in the capitals of powerful 🗺.

🧍 had spoken with many 🧍: with government administrators and 🎖 officers, 🧑 superintendents and corporate executives, 🎓

presidents and shop foremen, utility supervisors and foundation directors, with the 👤 of shops and stores, of 🏭 , 🏢 and 🏛 , with 😊 and 😴 young and 🙂 .

👤 had gone into every kind of 🏢 , large and small, luxurious and sparse, with windows and without.

👤 was beginning to 👁 the 🌈 spectrum of how 👥 manage 👥 .

Blithe wasn't always pleased with 😀 👤 saw.

👤 had seen many "tough" 👤 whose organizations seemed to 🏆 while their 👥 🏳 .

Some of their superiors thought 👫 were 👍 👤 .

Many of their subordinates thought otherwise.
As the 🐱 sat in each of these "tough people's" 🏢,
👤 asked, "😊 kind of a 👔 would 😊 say 😊 👉"?
Those to whom 👥 reported had their ✋.
As the 🐱 sat and listened to these "nice" 👫 ✅
the same ?, 👤 heard,

"I'm a 📓 👔". "Participative".
"Supportive". "Considerate". "Humanistic".
👤 heard the 😊 in their voices and their interest in
👫.
Their ✅ varied only slightly.

"I'm an autocratic 👔 😊 keep ↔️ 🔺 of the
situation", 👤 was told. "A bottom-line 👔". "Hard-nosed". "Realistic". "Profit-minded".
👤 heard the 😊 in their voices and their interest in
results.

The 🐱 also met many "nice" 👔 whose 👫
seemed to 🏆 while their organizations 📉.
Some of the 👫 who reported to them thought 👥
were 😊 👔.

But 🧑 was disturbed.

It was as though most 🧍 in the 🌐 were primarily interested either in results or in 👫 . The 🧍 who were interested in results often seemed to be labeled "autocratic", while the 🧍 interested in 👫 were often labeled "🏞" . The young 🐱 thought each of these 🧍, the "tough" autocrat and the "nice" democrat were only partially effective. "It's 😄 🅱 half a 🧍 ", 🧑 thought.

🧑 returned 👥 😟 and 🧑.

🧑 might 🔲 given 👍 👋 🔍 long ago, but 🧑 had 1️⃣ 🏴 advantage. 🧑 knew exactly 😶 🧑 was 👁 for.

"Effective 🧍 ", 🧑 thought, "manage themselves and the 👫 👬 👨‍👨‍👦 with 🆘 that both the organization and the 👫 profit from their presence".

The young 💀 had looked everywhere for an effective

🙎 but had found only a few. The few 🙎 did 🔍

would not share their 😊 with him. 🙎 began to 😟

maybe 🙎 would never 🔍 out 😟 really made an

effective 🙎 ✅.

Then 🙎 began 👂 marvelous stories about a special

🙎 who lived, ironically, in a nearby town. 🙎 heard

that 👯 liked to 📷 for this 💀 and that 📻

produced 🏆 results together. The young 💀 wondered

if the stories were really true and, if 🆘, whether this

🙎 would be willing to share 📝 😊 with him.

Curious, 🙎 telephoned the special manager's secretary

for an appointment. The secretary put him through

immediately.

The young 😊 asked this special 👤 when 👤 could

👁 him. 👤 heard, "Any ⌚ this week is fine, except

Wednesday 😊. 😄 🔨 the ⌚ ".

The young 😊 quietly chuckled because this supposedly

marvelous 👤 sounded 😊 a "kook" to him. 😊
kind of 👤 had that kind of ⌚ available? But the
young 😊 was fascinated. 👤 went to 👁 him.

The 1️⃣ Minute 👨

WHEN the young 🧒 arrived at the manager's 🏢, 🧑 found him standing and 👁 out of the window. When the young 🧒 coughed, the 👨 turned and smiled.

🧑 invited the young 🧒 to 🪑 🔼 and asked, "😀 can 😀 do for 😀"?

The young 🧒 said, "I'd 😀 to ask 😀 some ❓ about how 😀 manage 👫".

The 👨 willingly said. "🔥 away".

"Well, to begin with, do 😀 hold regularly scheduled meetings with your subordinates"?
"👍, 😀 do once a week 🔀 Wednesdays from 9:00 to 11:00. That's why

😀 couldn't 👁 😀 then", responded the 👨.

"😀 do 😀 do at those meetings"? probed the young 🧒.

13

"[emoji] [emoji] while my [emoji] review and analyze [emoji] [emoji]

accomplished last week, the [emoji] [emoji] had, and [emoji]

still needs to be accomplished. Then [emoji] develop plans

and strategies for the [emoji] week".

"[emoji] the decisions made at those meetings [emoji] [emoji]

both [emoji] and your [emoji] "? questioned the young [emoji].

"Of course [emoji] [emoji] ", insisted the [emoji]. "[emoji] would

be the [emoji] of [emoji] the meeting if [emoji] weren't"?

"Then [emoji] [emoji] a participative [emoji], aren't [emoji] "?' asked

the young [emoji].

"[emoji] the contrary", insisted the [emoji], "[emoji] don't believe

in participating in any of my people's decision-making".

"Then [emoji] is the purpose of your meetings"?

"[emoji] already told [emoji] that", [emoji] said. "[emoji], young [emoji], do not ask me to [🔁] myself. It is a waste of my [⌚] and yours.

"We're [📌] to [🏆] results", the [🧑] continued. "The purpose of this organization is efficiency. By [🅱️] organized [👓] [👉] a [💼] deal [➕] productive".

"Oh, [🆘] you're aware of the need for productivity. Then you're [➕] results-oriented than people-oriented", the young [👶] suggested.

"Xo"! the [🧑] resounded, [🆕] [✋] visitor "[😄] [🕯️] that all too often". [🧑] got to [👟] [🚶] and began to walk about. "How [↔️] [🌐] can [😊] [🏆] results if it's not through [👬]? [😊] care about [👬] and results. [👓] go [🤼] in [🤼].

"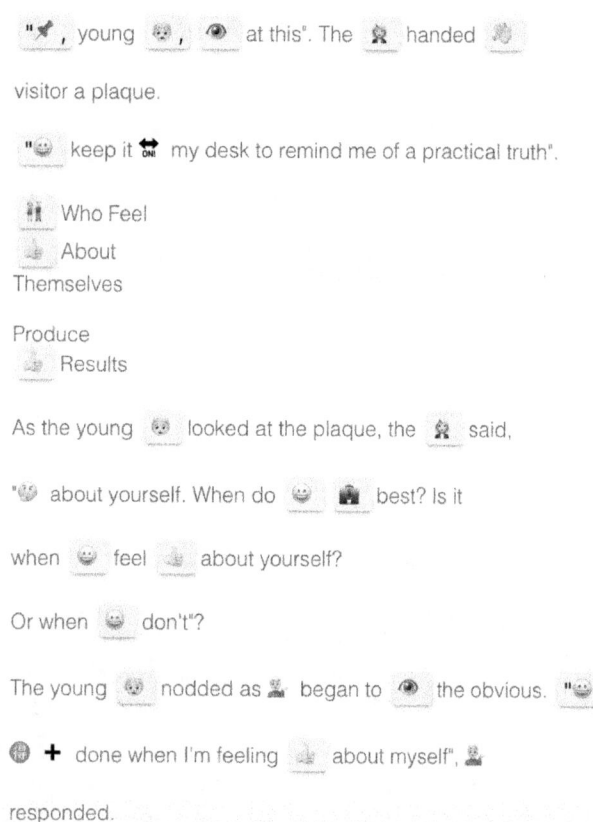, young 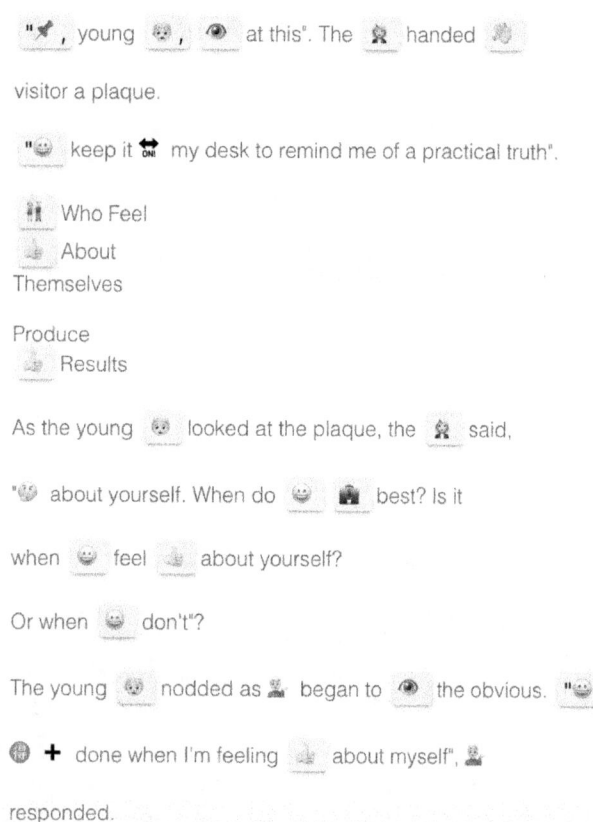, 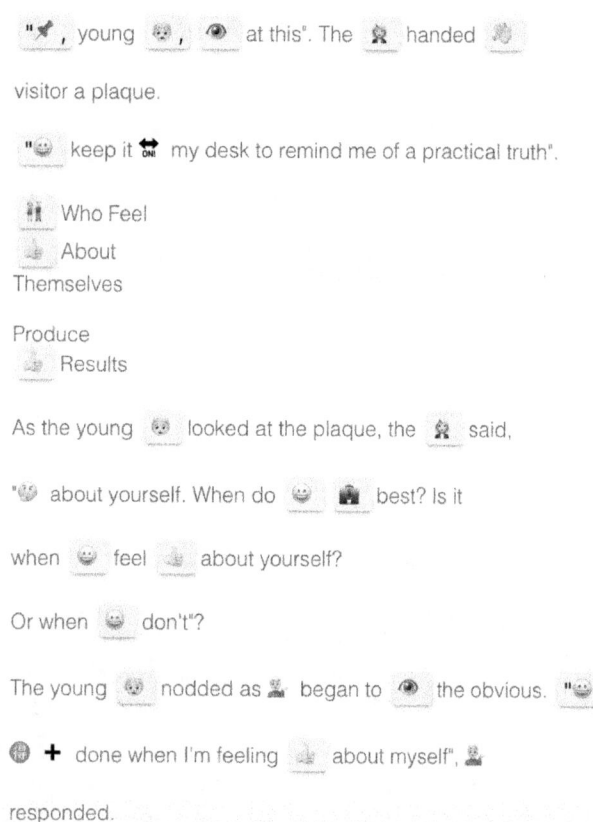 at this". The 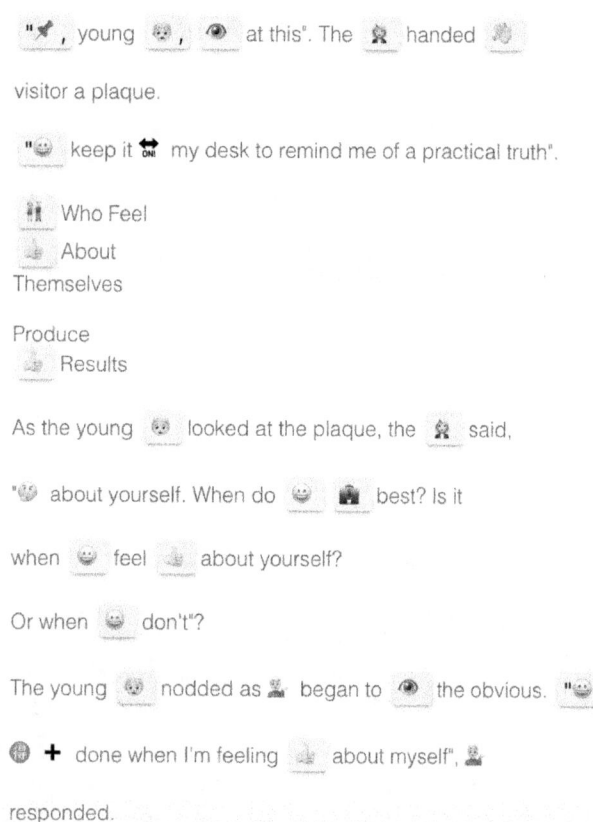 handed

visitor a plaque.

" keep it my desk to remind me of a practical truth".

 Who Feel
 About
Themselves

Produce
 Results

As the young looked at the plaque, the said,

" about yourself. When do   best? Is it

when feel about yourself?

Or when don't"?

The young nodded as began to the obvious. "

 + done when I'm feeling about myself",

responded.

"Of course 😊 do", the 🧑 agreed. "And 🆘 does

everyone else".

The young 😊 👆 👆 index 👆 with new-found

insight. "🆘 ", 🧑 said, "🆘 🚻 to feel 👍 about

themselves is a 🔑 to 🌐 ➕ done".

" 👍 ", the 🧑 agreed. "However, remember

productivity is ➕ than just the quantity of 🚗 done.

It is also the quality". 🧑 walked over to the window and

said, "Come over 📌 , young 😊 ".

🧑 pointed to the traffic below and asked, "Do 😊 👁

how many foreign 🚙 there 🔄 the 🚗 "?

The young 😊 looked out at the real 🌍 , and said, "😊

👁 ➕ of them every day. And 😊 guess that's because

they're ✚ economical and 👟👟 last longer".

The 🧍 nodded reluctantly and said "Exactly. 🆘 why do 😀 😁 🧑‍🤝‍🧑 ☞ 🏬 foreign 🚗?

Because 🤚 manufacturers did not make enough 🚙? Or", the 🧍 said without interrupting, "because 👟👟 did not make the quality 🚗 the 🤚 🏛️ really wanted?

"Now that 😀 😁 of it", the young 🐱 answered, "it's a ? of quality and quantity"

"Of course", the 🧍 added. "Quality is simply 🖼️ 🧑‍🤝‍🧑 the product or 🔔 👟👟 really want and need".

The older 🐱 stood at the window 📜 in 👐 thoughts. 🧍 could remember, not 🆘 long ago, when 🖐️ 📱 provided the 📖 that helped to rebuild Europe and 📷. It still amazed him that 📨 had fallen 🆘 far behind in productivity.

The young 💀 broke the manager's concentration. "I'm reminded of an ad 😃 saw ↔ 📺 ", the visitor volunteered. "It showed the name of the foreign 🚗 , and over it came the 🆔 If 😃 're going to take out a long-term 🚗 loan, don 't 🏢 a short-term 🚗 ".
The 👺 turned and said quietly, "I'm afraid that's a rather 👎 summary. And that's the whole 🟦 . Productivity is both quantity and quality".
The 👺 and 🔥 visitor began to walk 🔙 towards the couch. "And frankly, the best 🔼 to achieve both of these results is through 👫 ".

The young man's interest increased. As 👤 sat 🌱 , 👺 asked, "Well, you've already said that you're not a participative 👺 . Just how would 😃 describe yourself"?

"That's easy", 👤 responded without hesitation. "I'm a 1️⃣ Minute 👺 ".

The young man's 😃 showed 😳 . He'd never heard of a 1️⃣ Minute 👺 . "You're a 😶 "?

The 🧝 laughed and said, "I'm a 1️⃣ Minute 🧝. 😊 call myself that because it takes very little ⌚ for me to 🎯 very big results from 🚻".

Although the young 👶 had spoken with many 🧝, 👤 had never heard 1️⃣ 💬 😊 this. It was hard to believe. A 1️⃣ Minute 🧝 someone who 🎯 👐 results without taking much ⌚.

👁️ the 💃 🔛 👏 😊 the 🧝 said, "😊 don't believe me, do 😊? 😊 don't believe that I'm a 1️⃣ Minute 🧝".

"😊 must admit it's hard for me even to imagine", the young 👶 responded.

The 🧝 laughed and said, "🗨️, you'd better 💬

to my 👣 if 😊 really want to know 😮 kind of

🧍 😊 ☜ ".

The 🧍 leaned over and spoke into the 📠

intercom. 🙋 secretary, Ms. Metcalfe, came in moments

later and handed the young 😮 a sheet of 🖨.

"Those ☜ the names, positions and 📞 💯 of

the 6️⃣ 👣 who report to me", the 1️⃣ Minute

🧍 explained.

"Which 1️⃣ should 😊 💬 to"? the young 😮 asked.

"That's your decision", the 🧍 responded. "🔨 any

name. 💬 to anyone of them or all of them".

"Well, 😊 😄 who should 😊 🆕 with"?

"😊 already told 😊, 😊 don't make decisions for other

👥 ", the 🧙 said firmly. "Make that decision yourself". 🧑 stood 🕐 and walked 👋 visitor towards the 🔑 .

"😀 🏢 asked me, not once, but twice, to make a simple decision for 😊. Frankly, young 😊, 😊 🔍 that annoying. Do not ask me to 🔄 myself. Either 🔨 a name and 🉐 started, or take your 🔍 for effective management elsewhere".

The visitor was 😊 . 🧑 was uncomfortable, very uncomfortable. A moment of 😊 🗄 seemed 😀 an eternity.

Then the 1️⃣ Minute 🧙 looked the young 😊 in the 😊 and said,

"😊 want to know about managing 👥, and 😊 admire that". 🧑 shook 🤚 visitor's ✋.

"If 😊 🈂 any ❓ after 💬 to some of my 👥", 🧑 said warmly, "come 🔙 and 👁 me. 😊 appreciate your interest and desire to 🎓 how to manage. 😊 would, in fact, 😊 to give 😊 the concept of the 1️⃣ Minute 🧑 as a 🎁. Someone gave it to me once and it's made all the difference to me. 😊 want 😊 to understand it fully. If 😊 😊 it, 😊 may want to become a 1️⃣ Minute 🧑 yourself someday".

"Thank 😊", the young 🧑 managed.

🧑 🔜 the manager's 🏢 somewhat dumbfounded. As 🧑 passed the secretary 🧑 said understandingly, "😊 can

👁 from your dazed 👁 that you've already experienced

our 1️⃣ Minute 🐀 ".

The young 🐱 said very slowly, still 🔵 to figure

🐘 out, "😊 guess 😊 📒 ".

"Maybe 😊 can 🆘 😊 ", Ms. Metcalfe said. "I've phoned

the 6️⃣ 👫 who report to him. 5️⃣ of them ☞ 🪁

and 👯 🎴 each agreed to 👁 😊. 😊 may be better

able to understand our '1️⃣ Minute 🐀 ' after

you've spoken with them".

The young 🐱 thanked her, looked over the list and

decided to 💬 to 3️⃣ of them: Mr. Trenell, Mr. Levy

and Ms. 🐿 .

The 🥇 😊 : 1️⃣ Minute Goals

WHEN the young 😺 arrived at Trenell's 🏢, 🧑 found a 😊 😊 at him. "Well, you've been to 👁 the 'ole 😺 ". He's quite a 😊, isn't 🧑 "?

"🧑 seems that ⬆️ ", the young 😺 responded.

"Did 🧑 tell 😊 about 🅱️ a 1️⃣ Minute 🕺 '? :

"🧑 sure did. It's not true, is it"? asked the young 😺.

"You'd better believe it is. 😊 hardly ever 👁 him".

"😺 😊 😊 never 🈶 any 🆘 from him"? puzzled the young 😺.

"Essentially very little, although 🧑 does spend some ⌚ with me at the beginning of a 🆕 task or responsibility. That's when 🧑 does 1️⃣ Minute Goal Setting". "1️⃣ Minute Goal Setting. What's that"? said the young 😺.

"👤 told me 👤 was a 1️⃣ Minute 👥, but 👤 didn't

say anything about 1️⃣ Minute Goal Setting".

"That's the 🔑 of the 3️⃣ 😀 to 1️⃣ Minute

Management", Tienell answered.

"3️⃣ 😀"? the young 😀 asked, wanting to know

➕.

"👣", said Tienell. "1️⃣ Minute Goal Setting is the 🔑

1️⃣ and the foundation for 1️⃣ Minute Management. 😀

👁, in most organizations when 😀 ask 👬 😀 👭

do and then ask their boss, all too often 😀 🏢 ✌️

different lists. In fact, in some organizations I've worked

in, any relationship between 😀 😀 thought my job

responsibilities were and 😀 my boss thought 👭

were, was purely coincidental. And then 😃 would 🎯 in

trouble for not doing something 😃 didn't even 🌀 was

my job".

"Does that ever happen 🔑"? asked the young 😈.

"🌀"! Trenell said. "It never happens 🔑. The 1️⃣

Minute 🏃 always makes it clear 😃 our

responsibilities ✏️ and 😃 👀 ✏️ B held

accountable for".

"Just how does 🏃 do that"? the young 😈 wanted to

know.

"Efficiently", Trenell said with a 😃.

Trenell began to explain. "Once 🏃 has told me 😃

needs to be done or 👀 📋 agreed 🔀 😃 needs to be

done, then each goal is recorded 🔀 😃 ➕ than a 📇

page. The 1 Minute 🧍 feels that a goal, and its

performance standard, should take 🙁 ✚ than 250

🆔 to 🚚 . 🧍 insists that anyone be able to 🚗 it

within a minute. 🧍 keeps a copy and 🙂 keep a copy 🆘

everything is clear and 🆘 👥 can both periodically check

the 🎞️ .

"Do 🙂 📝 these one-page statements for every goal"?

" 🙅 ", answered Trenell.

"Well, wouldn't there be a lot of these one-page

statements for each 👤 "?

" 🙂 , there really aren't", Trenell insisted. "The 👶 👶

believes in the 80-20 goal-setting 🚧 . That is, 🔢 % of

your really important results will come from 20% of your

goals. 🆘 👭 only do 1️⃣ Minute Goal Setting 🔛 that

20,% that is, our 🔑 areas of responsibility maybe 3️⃣
to 6️⃣ goals in all. Of course, in the 🖼 a special project
comes 🕐, 👭 set special 1️⃣ Minute Goals".
"Interesting", the young 🐵 commented. "🐵 👀 😊
understand the importance of 1️⃣ Minute Goal Setting. It
🌱 😊 a philosophy of '🐵 😺' — everyone
knows 😊 is expected from the beginning "
"Exactly", Trenell nodded.
"🆘 is 1️⃣ Minute Goal Setting just understanding 😊
your responsibilities ☞"? the young 🐵 asked.
"😺. Once 👭 know 😊 our job is, the 🧛 always
makes sure 👭 know 😊 👎 performance is. In other
🆔, performance standards ☞ clear. 🧛 📺 us
😊 🧛 expects".
"How does 🧛 do that — 📺 😊 😊 🧛 expects"?

asked the young 🐱.

29

"Let me give 🙂 an example", Trenell suggested.

1️⃣ of my 1️⃣ Minute Goals was this: Identify performance ⚠️ and come 🔆 with solutions which, when implemented, will turn the situation around.

"When 🙂 🔆 came to 🏢 📌 🙂 spotted a ⚠️ that needed to be solved, but 🙂 didn't know 👀 to do. 🆘 🙂 called the 1️⃣ Minute 👤.

When 🧍 answered the ☎️, 🙂 said, 🐯, 🙂 🎞️ a ⚠️. Before 🙂 could 🔘 another 🆔 out, 🧍 said, 👍! That's 👀 you've been hired to solve.

Then there was a 💀 📲 ⚡ the other 🔚 of the ☎️.

"🙂 didn't know 👀 to do. The 📱 was deafening. 🙂 eventually stuttered out, But, but, 🐯, 🙂 don't know how to solve this ⚠️.

"Trenell, 🧍 said, 1️⃣ of your goals for the 📆 is for 🙂 to identify and solve your own ⚠️. But since 🙂 ⬅️ 📱, come ⚡ 🔆 and we'll 💬.

"When 😊 got 👉 there, 🧑 said, Tell me, Trenell, 😟 your

⚠ is — but put it in behavioral terms.

"Behavioral terms? 😊 echoed. 😟 do 😊 😟 by

behavioral terms?

"😊 😟 , the 🧑 explained to me, that 😊 do not want

to 🗨 about only attitudes or feelings. Tell me 😟 is

happening in observable, measurable terms.

"😊 described the ⚠ the best 😊 could.

"🧑 said, That's 👍, Trenell! Now tell me 😟 yon

would 😊 to be happening in behavioral terms.

"I don't know," 😊 said.

"Then don't waste my ⌚, 🧑 snapped.

"😊 just froze in amazement for a few ⏱ . 😊 didn't

know 😟 to do.

🧑 mercifully broke the 😵 🔲 .

"If 😊 can't tell me 😟 you'd 😊 to be happening, 🧑

said, 😊 don't 🔲 a ⚠ yet. You're just

complaining. A ⚠ only exists if there is a difference

between 😟 is actually happening and 😟 😊 desire

to be happening.

"🅱 a quick learner, 😊 suddenly realized 😊 knew 😟 1️⃣

wanted to be happening. After 😊 told him, 🧑 asked me to

💬 about 😟 may 🔲 caused the discrepancy between

the actual and the desired.

"After that the ☝ Minute 🙋 said. Well, 😀 what 😀 going to do about it?"

"Well, 😀 could do A, 😀 said.

"If 😀 did A, would 😀 😀 want to happen actually happen?" 🙋 asked.

"😟, 😀 said.

"Then 😀 😀 a lousy solution. 😀 else could 😀 do?" 🙋 asked.

"😀 could do B," 😀 said.

"But if 😀 do B, will 😀 😀 want to happen really happen?" 🙋 countered again.

"😟, 😀 realized.

"Then, that's also a 🗒 solution, 🙋 said. 😀 else can 😀 do?"

"😀 thought about it for a 🕐 of minutes and said, 😀 could do C. But if 😀 do C, 😀 😀 want to happen won't happen, 🆘 that is a 🗒 solution, isn't it!" "👍. You're 🔪 to come around," the 🙋 then said, with a 😀 ↔ 💤 😀. Is there anything else 😀 could do? 🙋 asked.

"Maybe 😀 could combine some of these solutions, 😀 said

"That 💡 worth 🎬, 🙋 reacted.

"In fact, if 😊 do A this week, B ⏭ week and C in 😊 weeks, I'll 🖼 it solved. That's fantastic. 🙌 sos much. 😊 solved my ⚠ for me.

😾 got very 😠 . 😊 did not, 😾 interrupted, 😊 solved it yourself. 😊 just asked 😄 ? — ?

😊 ☞ able to ask yourself. Now 🔄 out of 📌 and 🆕 solving your own ⚠ ↔ your 🔋 , not mine.

"😊 knew 😊 😾 had done, of course. He'd shown me how to solve ⚠ sos that 😊 could do it ↔ my own in the 🏫 .

"Then 😾 stood, looked me straight in the 😊 and said. You're 👍, Trenell. Remember that the ⏭ 🔋 😊 🈁 a ⚠ .

"😊 remember 😊 as 😊 🔄 🌸 📷 ". Trenell leaned 🔙 in 🌸 chair and looked as if 😾 were reliving 🌸 🏅 encounter with the 1 Minute 👮 .

"sos ", the young 😊 began, reflecting ↔ 😊 😾 had just heard....

Minute Goals: Summary

Minute Goal Setting is simply:

1. your goals.

2. behavior .

3. out each of your goals a sheet of — than 250 .

4. and re-read each goal, which requires only minute or each do it.

5. Take a minute every once in a while out of your day to at your performance, and

6. whether or not your behavior matches your goal.

"That's it", Trenell exclaimed, "you're a   learner".

"Thank   ", the young   said, feeling   about himself. "But let me just jot that   ",   said, "   want to remember that".

After the young   wrote briefly in the small

      carried with him,   leaned   and asked, "If   Minute Goal Setting is the   to becoming a   Minute   ,   the other   "?

Trenell smiled, looked at   and said, "Why don't   ask Levy that?   scheduled to   him this   too, aren't   "?

The young   was amazed. How did Trenell know that?

"   ", the young   said as   to   Trenell's   . "   much for your   ,   "

"You're welcome", Trenell answered. "   is   a lot   of now. As   can probably tell, I'm becoming a   Minute   myself".

The 🐰 😊: 1️⃣ Minute Praisings

As the young 😊 🐭 Trenell's 🏢, 🧑 was struck by the simplicity of 😊 🧑 had heard. 🧑 thought, "It certainly makes sense. After all, how can 😊 be an effective 🧑 unless 😊 and your 🧑 ☞ sure of 😊 👬 ☞ B asked to do. And 😊 an efficient 🕹️ to do it".

The young 🐱 walked the 🔪 of the 🧸 and took the elevator to the 🐰 🏢. When 🧑 got to Mr. Levy's 🏢, 🧑 was 😊 to meet 🆘 young a 😊.

Levy was probably in 🤚 🕐 20's or 🕐 30's. "Well, you've been to 👁️ the 'ole 😊'. He's quite a 😊, isn't 🧑 "?

🧑 was already geitting used to the 1️⃣ Minute 🧑 B called "quite a 😊".

"😊 guess 🧑 is", responded the young 😊.

"Did 🧑 tell 😊 about B a 1️⃣ Minute 🧑 "? asked Levy.

"🧑 sure did. It's not true, is it"? asked the young 🐱, wondering if he'd 🔟 a different ☑️ from Trenell's.

"😀 😐 😊 never 🏦 any 🆘 from him"? pursued the young 🐹.

"Essentially very little, although 👨‍💼 does spend a fair amount of ⌚ with me at the beginning of a 🆕 task or responsibility".

"👍, 😊 know about 1️⃣ Minute Goal Setting", interrupted the young 😣.

"Actually 😊 wasn't 😐 🆘 much about 1️⃣ Minute Goal Setting. 😊 was referring to 1️⃣ Minute Praisings".

"1️⃣ Minute Praisings"? echoed the young 🐹. "👉 👟 the 🔑 😊 to becoming a 1️⃣ Minute 🧝"?

"👍, 😊 👞", Levy revealed. "In fact, when 😀 🧝 started to 🏢 📌, the 1️⃣ Minute 🧝 made it very clear to me 😐 👨‍💼 was going to do"

"😮 was that"? the visitor asked.

"👨‍💼 said that 👨‍💼 knew that it would be a lot easier for me to do well, if 😊 got crystal-clear feedback from him ↔️ how 😊 was doing.

"👨‍💼 said 👨‍💼 wanted me to succeed. 👨‍💼 wanted me to be a big 🆘 to the organization, and to enjoy my 💼.

"👨‍💼 told me that 👨‍💼 would try, therefore, to let me know

"And then 👤 cautioned me that it might not be very comfortable at 🥇 for either of us".

"Why"? the visitor asked.

"Because, as 👤 pointed out to me then, most 👥 don't manage that 📥 and 👫 aren't used to it. Then 👤 assured me that such feedback would be a big 🆘 too.

"Can 😊 give me an example of 😊 😊 ☞ 💬 about"? the young 😺 requested.

"Sure", Levy complied. "Shortly after 😊 started to 🔭 , 😊 noticed that, after my 👤 had done 1️⃣ Minute Goal Setting with me, 👤 would stay in close contact".

"😺 do 😊 😺 by 'close contact"?' asked the young 😺 .

"There were 🥇 📥 that 👤 did it", explained Levy.

" 🥇 of all, 👤 observed my activities very closely. 👤 never seemed to be very far away. Secondly, 👤 made me keep detailed 🎬 of my 🎞️ which 👤 insisted 😊 send to him".

"That's interesting", said the young 😺 . "Why does 👤 do that"?

"At 🥇 😊 thought 👤 was 👹 and didn't trust me. That is, until 😊 found out from some of the other 👫 who report to him 😺 👤 was really doing".

"😊 was that"? the young 😺 wanted to know.

"🖼 was 📷 to catch me doing something 👉 ", Levy said.

"Catch 😄 doing something 👉 "? echoed the young 🐱.

"🔩 ", responded Levy. "👀 📇 a motto around 📌 that says:

🆘 👫
Reach Their
🈵 Potential
Catch Them
Doing Something
👉

Levy continued, "In most organizations the 👤 spend most of their 👜 catching 👫 doing 😠 "? 👤 asked the young 🐱.

The young 😺 smiled and said knowingly, "Doing something wrong".

"👉 "! said Levy, "🏌 👀 put the accent 🔛 the positive. 👀 catch 👫 doing something 👉 ".

The young 😺 made a few 📖 in 🤚 📷 and then asked, "😊 happens, Mr. Levy, when the 1️⃣ Minute 👤 catches 😄 doing something right"

"That's when 🖼 gives 😄 a 1️⃣ Minute 👏 ", Levy

said with some delight.

"🙂 does that 😆"? the young 😠 wanted to know.

"Well, when 🧑 has seen that 🙂 🖼 done something

👍, 🧑 comes over and makes contact with 🙂. That

often includes putting 🤚 🙌 🔀 your shoulder or briefly

touching 🙂 in a friendly 🔵".

"Doesn't that bother 🙂", the young 😠 wondered,

"when 🧑 touches 🙂"?

"😒"! Levy insisted. "🔀 the contrary, it 🆘. 🙂 know 🧑

really cares about me and 🧑 wants me to prosper. As 🧑

says, the ➕ consistently successful your 👥 👍, the

higher 🙂 rise in the organization".

"When 🧑 makes contact, it's brief, but it lets me know

once again that we're really 🔀 the same side.

"Anyway, after that", Levy continued, "🧑 👁 🙂

straight in the 🙂 and tells 🙂 precisely 🙂 🙂 did

👍. Then 🧑 shares with 🙂 how 👍 🧑 feels about

🙂 🙂 did".

"🙂 don't 😕 I've ever heard of a 🦁 doing that",

the young 😠 broke in. "That must make 🙂 feel pretty

👍".

"It certainly does", Levy confirmed, "for several reasons.

🥇 of all, 😀 🏅 a ✋ as ➡SOON as I've done

something 👉 " 👨 smiled and leaned towards 🧑

visitor. Then 👨 laughed and said, "😀 don't 📖 to ☝

for an annual performance review, if 😀 know 😄 😄

😄 ". Both 😀 smiled.

"🥇 , since 👨 specifies exactly 😀 did 👉 , 😄

know he's sincere and familiar with 😄 😄 👉 doing.

🥇 , 👨 is consistent".

"Consistent"? echoed the young 😄 , wanting to know

➕ .

" 👨 ", insisted Levy. "👨 will ✋ me if 😀 👉

performing well and deserve it even if 🐘 👉 not

going well for him elsewhere. 😀 know 👨 may be 😄

about other 🐘 . But 👨 responds to where 😀 👉 , not

just to where 👨 is at the ⌚ . And 😀 really appreciate

that".

"Doesn't all this ✋ 📖 to take 👆 a lot of the

manager's ⌚ "? the young 😄 asked.

"Not really", said Levy. "Remember 😀 don't 📖 to

✋ someone for very long for them to know 😀

noticed and 😀 care. It usually takes ➖ than a minute".

"And that's why it's called a 📖 Minute ✋ ", the

visitor said, as 👤 wrote 🔑 😊 👤 was 🎓.

"📟", Levy said.

"Is 👤 always 📱 to catch 😊 doing something 👉"? the young 🐭 asked.

"🙀, of course not", Levy answered. "Just when 😊 💰 🆕 📷 📌 or when 😊 begin a 🆕 project or responsibility, then 👤 does. After 😊 🏦 to know the ropes, 👤 doesn't seem to be around much".

"Why"? the young 🐭 wondered.

"Because 😊 and 👤 🏦 other 🆙 of knowing when your job performance is 'praiseworthy'. 😊 both can review the 🅲 in the 👤 system: the 🍞 figures, expenditures, production 📅, and 🆘 ↔. And then", Levy added, "after awhile 😊 begin to catch yourself doing 🦬 👉 and 😊 🆕 👏 yourself.

Also, you're always wondering when 👤 might 👏 😊 again and that seems to keep 😊 going even when he's not around. It's uncanny. I've never worked 🆘 hard at a job in my life "

"That's really interesting", commented the young 🐭.

"🆘 1️⃣ Minute 👏 is a 😊 to becoming a 1️⃣ Minute 👤 ".

42

"It is, indeed", Levy said with a gleam in 👋 😊. 👤 enjoyed 👁 someone 🎓 the 😊 of 1️⃣ Minute Management.

As the visitor looked at 👋 📕, 👤 quickly reviewed 😊 👤 had learned about the 1️⃣ Minute 👏.

1️⃣ Minute 👏 : Summary

The 1️⃣ Minute 👏 📷 well when 😊 :

1️⃣. Tell 🧍 👆 front that 😊 ☜ going to let them know how 👥 ☜ doing.

2️⃣. 👏 🧍 immediately.

😕. Tell 🧍 😊 👥 did ☜ & be specific.

4️⃣. Tell 🧍 how 👍 😊 feel about 😊 👥 did ☜, and how it 🆘 the organization and the other 🧍 who 📷 there.

5️⃣. 🤚 for a moment of 🤫 to let them "feel" how 👍 😊 feel.

6️⃣. Encourage them to do ➕ of the same.

7️⃣. 👋 🤝 or touch 🧍 in a 🔄 that makes it clear that 😊 λ their 📈 in the organization.

43

"What's the 🏅 😊"? the young 😀 asked anxiously.

Levy laughed at the visitor's enthusiasm, 🏋 from 🪑 chair and said, "Why don't 😀 ask Ms. 🦫 ? 😀 understand you're 📆 to 💬 to her, too".

" 🍂 , 😀 👉 ", admitted the young 😀 . "Well, 🙌 🆘 much for your 🏒 ".

"That's 👌 ", insisted Levy. " ⌚ is 1️⃣ 🐘 😀 🔢 plenty of, 😀 👁 I'm a 1️⃣ Minute 🐿 myself now".

The visitor smiled. He'd heard that somewhere before. 🐈 wanted to reflect 🔛 😀 🐈 was 🎓 . 🐈 🍂 the 🐿 and took a walk among the 🌿 nearby. 🐈 was struck again by the simplicity and common sense of 😀 🐈 had heard. "How can 😀 argue with the effectiveness of catching 👫 doing something 👉 ". the young 😀 thought, "especially after 🙈 know 😀 🙈 👉 to do and 😀 👍 performance 👁 😀 .

"But do 1️⃣ Minute Praisings really 🐒 "? 🐈 wondered. "Does all this 1️⃣ Minute Management stuff really 🌐 results — bottom-line results"?

As 🧑 walked along 🏢 curiosity about results increased.

🆘 🧑 returned to the 1️⃣ Minute Manager's secretary

and asked Ms. Metcalfe to reschedule 🗓 appointment

with Ms. 🐍 for some 🕐 the 📶 🔆 .

"Tomorrow 🙂 is fine", the secretary said as 🧑

hung 👆 the ☎ . "Ms. 🐍 said to tell 😃 to come

any 🕐 except Wednesday 🙂 ".

Then 🧑 called 🖼 and made the 🆕

appointment 🧑 requested. 🧑 was to 👁 Ms. Gomez, an

official in the headquarters 🏢 . 👀 🔲

🧑 there about all the different 👇 and

🎌 in the total company", Ms. Metcalfe said in a

very knowing 🎲 . "I'm sure you'll 🔍 whatever you're

👁 for". 🧑 thanked her and 🔜 .

The Appraisal

AFTER ▢ the young 😺 went ▰ . 👤 met
with Ms. Gomez, a competent 👁 👤 in her 🕐
40's. 🍔 🔌 to 🙇 , the young 😺 asked,
"Could 😄 🙏 tell me 😃 is the most efficient and
effective of all your operations in the 🔪 ? 😄 want to
compare it with the so-called '1️⃣ Minute Manager's'. "
A moment later, 👤 laughed, as 👤 heard Ms. Gomez say,
"Well, 😄 won't 🎴 to 👁 very far, because it is the
1️⃣ Minute Manager's. He's quite a 😺, isn't 👤 ? 🌀
operation is the most efficient and effective of all of our
plants."
"That's unbelievable", said the young 😺 . "Does 👤
🎴 the best equipment'.'?
"😵 ", said Ms. Gomez. "In fact, he's got some of the
oldest".
"Well, there's got to be something wrong out there", said
the young 😺, still puzzled by the 😺 man's
management 📏 . "Tell me, does 👤 lose a lot of 🌀
🍴 ? Does 👤 🎴 a lot of turnover"?
"Come to 😵 of it", Ms. Gomez said, "👤 does 🎴 a
lot of turnover".

"Aha", the young 🐻 said, 😊 👤 was 🔛 to something.

"😌 happens to those folks when 👥 ✂️ the 1️⃣ Minute 🎯"? the young 🐻 wanted to know.

"👥 give them their own operation", Ms. Gomez quickly responded. "After 🕐 years with him, 👥 say, 'Who needs a 🎯'? He's our best trainer of 👫. Whenever 👥 📺 an 🌐 and need a 🛠️ 🎯, 👥 call him. 👤 always has somebody who is ready".

Amazed, the young 🐻 thanked Ms. Gomez for her 🔋, but this 🔋 👤 got a different response.

"😌 was 😊 😊 could fit 😊 in today", 👤 said. "The 😊 of my week is really jammed. 😊 🙏 😊 knew 🌐 the 1️⃣ Minute Manager's 😊 were. I've been 😊 to go over there and 👁️ him, but 😊 just haven't had 🕐".

😊, the young 🐻 said, "I'll give 😊 those 😊 as a 🎁 when 😊 🔍 them out myself. Just 😊 he's 👤 them to me".

"That would be a precious 🎁", Ms. Gomez said with a 😊. 👤 looked around her cluttered 🖼️ and said, "😊 could use whatever 🆘 😊 can 🔘".

The young 🐻 👋 Ms. Gomez's 🖼️ and walked out

onto the street, 🕊 🐝 🐿. The 1 Minute 👤 was absolutely fascinating to him.

That 🌙 the young 💀 had a very restless 🌑. 👤 found himself excited about the 📅 day; about 💎 the ⚫ 😊 to becoming a 1 Minute 👤.

The 🏅 😟 : 1️⃣ Minute Reprimands

THE ⏭️ 🙂 👤 arrived at Ms. Brown's 🏢 at the stroke of 9️⃣. A very smartly dressed 👩 in her 🕐 50's greeted him. 👤 got the usual, "He's quite a 🙂, isn't 👤"? routine, but by now the young 🙂 was 🉐 to the 📇 where 👤 could sincerely say, "👍, 👤 is"!

"Did 👤 tell 🙂 about 🅱️ a 1️⃣ Minute 👹"? asked Ms. 🐴.

"That's all I've been 👁 about", the young 🙂 said 😊. "It's not true, is it"? 👤 asked, still wondering if he'd 🉐 a different ✅.

"You'd better believe it is. 🙂 hardly ever 👁 him".

"🙂 😊 🙂 don't 🈶 much contact with him", pursued the young 🙂, "outside your regular weekly meeting"?

"Essentially very little. Except of course, when 🙂 do something wrong", said Ms. 🐴.

Shocked, the young 🙂 said, "🙂 😊 the only 🕴️ 🙂 👁 the 1️⃣ Minute 👹 is when 🙂 do something wrong"?

"👍. Well, not quite", said Ms. 🐴, "but almost".

"But 😀 thought a 🔑 motto around 🦴 was catching 👫 doing 🐃 🐁 "

"It is", insisted 🐿️ . "But 😀 📕 to know some 🐘 about me".

"😵 "? asked the young 🐥 .

"I've been 💼 📌 for quite a few years. 😀 know this operation inside and out. As a result, the 1️⃣ Minute 🐒 doesn't 📗 to spend much 🍗 with me, if any, 🔛 goal setting. In fact, 😀 usually ✍️ out my goals and send them over to him".

"Is each goal 🔛 a separate sheet of 🏛️ "? asked the young 🐥 .

"😀 🏛️ . 🐥 longer than 250 🆔 and each 1️⃣ takes me or the 1️⃣ Minute 🐒 only a minute to 🎮 .

"Another 🐘 about me that's important is that 😀 just 😍 my 💼 . As a result, 😀 do most of my own 1️⃣ Minute Praisings. In fact, 😀 believe if you're not for yourself, who is? A 💀 of mine told me a motto I'll always remember: 'If 😀 don't blow your own 👹 , someone else will use it as a spittoon'. "

The young 🐥 smiled. 🛏️ liked her sense of humor.

"Does your 🐒 ever 🔔 😀 "? 🛏️ asked.

"Sometimes 👤 does, but 👤 doesn't 📖 to do it very often because 😊 beat him to the punch", answered Ms. 🐾 . "When 😊 do something especially 👍, 😊 might even even ask the 1️⃣ Minute 👤 for a 🦪 ."

"How would 😊 ever 📖 the nerve to do that"? asked the young 🐶.

"It's easy. Just 😊 🚩 a 🏛 where 😊 either 🏆 or 😊 💚 even. If 👤 gives me the 🦪, 😊 🏆".

"But if 👤 doesn't"? the young 🐶 broke in.

"Then 😊 💚 even", responded Ms. 🐾 . "😊 didn't 📖 it before 😊 asked "

The young 🐶 smiled as 👤 took 📘 of Ms. Brown's philosophy, and then continued.

"😊 said 👤 spends ⌚ with 😊 when 😊 do something wrong. 🐶 do 😊 😊"? asked the young 🐶.

"If 😊 make a significant mistake, that's when 😊 invariably 🔔 a 1️⃣ Minute Reprimand", Ms. 🐾 said.

"A 😕"? the startled young 🐶 asked.

"A 1️⃣ Minute Reprimand", Ms. 🐾 repeated.

"That's the 🗝 😕 to becoming a 1️⃣ Minute 👤 ".

"How does it [emoji]"? wondered the young [emoji] out loud.

"It's simple", said Ms. [emoji].

"[emoji] figured you'd say that", said the young [emoji].

Ms. [emoji] joined [emoji] [emoji] and explained, "If [emoji] [emoji] been doing a job for some [emoji] and [emoji] know how to do it well, and [emoji] make a mistake, the [emoji] Minute [emoji] is quick to respond".

"[emoji] does [emoji] do"? asked the young [emoji].

"As soon as [emoji] has learned about the mistake [emoji] comes to [emoji] me. [emoji] [emoji] [emoji] the facts. Then [emoji] might put [emoji] [emoji] [emoji] my shoulder or maybe just come around to my side of the desk"

"Doesn't that bother [emoji]"? asked the young [emoji].

"Sure, it does, because [emoji] know what's [emoji], especially since [emoji] doesn't [emoji] a [emoji] [emoji] [emoji] [emoji]. "[emoji] [emoji] me straight in the [emoji]", [emoji] continued, "and tells me precisely [emoji] [emoji] did wrong. Then [emoji] shares with me how [emoji] feels about it — he's [emoji], [emoji], [emoji] or whatever [emoji] is feeling".

"How long does that take"? asked the young [emoji].

"Only about 30 [emoji] but sometimes it seems forever to me", confided Ms. [emoji].

The visitor couldn't [icon] but remember the feelings [icon]
had when the [1] Minute [icon] told him "in [icon]
uncertain terms" how [icon] [icon] was with [icon] indecision.

"And then [icon] happens"? the young [icon] asked as [icon]
moved to the edge of [icon] chair.

"[icon] lets [icon] [icon] said sink in with a few [icon] of
[icon] — [icon], does it sink in"!

"Then [icon] "? the young [icon] asked.

"[icon] [icon] me squarely in the [icon] and lets me know how
competent [icon] [icon] [icon] usually [icon] . [icon] makes sure [1]
understand that the only reason [icon] is [icon] with me is that
[icon] has [icon] much respect for me. [icon] says [icon] knows this is
[icon] unlike me. [icon] says how much [icon] [icon] [icon] to
[icon] me some other [icon], as long as [icon] understand that [icon]
does not welcome that same mistake again".

The young [icon] broke in. "It must make [icon] [icon] twice".

"It certainly does", Ms. [icon] nodded vigorously.

The young [icon] knew [icon] Ms. [icon] was [icon] about.

[icon] was taking [icon] now as [icon] as [icon] could. [icon] sensed
that it wasn't going to take this [icon] long to cover
several important [icon].

"[emoji] of all", Ms. [emoji] said, "[emoji] usually gives me the reprimand as [emoji] as I've done something wrong. [emoji], since [emoji] specifies exactly [emoji] [emoji] did wrong, [emoji] know [emoji] is '[emoji] [emoji] of [emoji]' and that I'm not going to [emoji] away with sloppiness. [emoji], since [emoji] doesn't [emoji] me as a [emoji] — only my behavior — it's easier for me not to become defensive. [emoji] don't try to rationalize away my mistake by [emoji] blame [emoji] him or somebody else. [emoji] know [emoji] is [B] fair. And fourth, [emoji] is consistent".

"Does that [emoji] [emoji] will reprimand [emoji] for doing something wrong, even if [emoji] [emoji] going well for him elsewhere"?

"[emoji]", [emoji] answered.

"Does the whole process really take only a minute"? the young [emoji] asked.

"Usually", [emoji] said. "And when it's over, it's over. A [1] Minute Reprimand doesn't last long but [emoji] can guarantee [emoji], [emoji] don't forget it, and [emoji] don't usually make the same mistake twice".

"[emoji] [emoji] [emoji] know [emoji] you're [emoji] about", the young [emoji] said. "I'm afraid [emoji] asked him ..."

"[emoji] [emoji]", [emoji] interrupted, "[emoji] didn't ask him to [emoji] himself".

The young [emoji] was [emoji]. "[emoji] did", [emoji] confessed.

"Then 😊 know 😕 it's 😊 to be 🔛 the receiving 🔚 of a 1️⃣ Minute Reprimand", 🧍 said. "Although 😊 expect, as a visitor, 😊 got a rather mild 1️⃣ ".

"😊 don't know if you'd call it mild", 🧍 said, "but 😊 don't 😕 I'll ask him to 🔁 himself very often. That was a mistake.

"😊 wonder", the visitor said out loud, "if the 1️⃣ Minute 🧘 ever makes a mistake. 🧍 seems almost too 💯 ".

Ms. 🐚 began to 😊. "Hardly", 🧍 said. "But 🧍 does 🀄 a 👍 sense of humor. 🆘 when 🧍 does make a mistake, 😊 forgetting to do the last half of the 1️⃣ Minute Reprimand, 👬 🔲 it out to him and kid him about it.

"After we've had ⌚ to recover from the Reprimand, that is. 👬 might, for example, 📞 him later and tell him 👬 know 👬 were wrong. Then 👬 might 😊 and ask for the 🌓 half of the Reprimand, because we're not feeling too 📉 ".

"And 😕 does 🧍 do then"? the young 🧑 asked.

"🧍 usually 😊 and says he's 💜 🧍 forgot to remind me that 😊 ☞ an 👌 🧍 ".

"🙂 can 😄 about praisings and reprimands"? the young 👹 asked.

"Sure", Ms. 🐴 said. "😄 👁️, the 1️⃣ Minute 🧑 has taught us the value of Ⓑ able to 😄 at ourselves when 👀 make a mistake. It 🆘 us 😳 ↔️ with our 💼".

"That's terrific", the young 👹 enthused. "How did 😄 🎓 to do that"?

"Simply", Ms. 🐴 answered, "by 👁️ the boss do it himself".

"😄 👅 your boss can 😄 at himself when 🧑 makes a mistake"? the 😳 young 👹 asked.

"Well, not always", Ms. 🐴 admitted. "He's 😄 most of us. Sometimes it's tough. But 🧑 often can. And when 🧑 does 😄 at himself, it has a positive effect ↔️ everyone around him".

"🧑 must be pretty secure", the young 👹 suggested.

"🧑 is", Ms. 🐴 answered.

The young 👹 was 😊. 🧑 was beginning to 👁️ how valuable such a 🧑 was to an organization.

"Why do 😄 👹 the 1️⃣ Minute Manager's reprimands 🔸 🆘 effective"? 🧑 asked.

"I'll let 😊 ask the 1️⃣ Minute 🐿 ", 👤 said, as

👤 📛 from behind the desk and walked the young 😐

to the 🚪.

When 👤 thanked her for her ⌚, Ms. 🐚 smiled and

said, "😊 know 😐 the response to that is going to be".

🔭 both laughed. 👤 was beginning to feel 😊 an

"insider" rather than a visitor, and that felt ⭐.

As ➡️ as 👤 was in the hall, 👤 realized how little ⌚

he'd 😵 with her and how much 👤 👤 had

given him.

👤 reflected ↔️ 😐 👤 had said. It sounded 🆘 simple.

👤 reviewed in 🔥 own mind 😐 😊 should do when

😐 catch an experienced 👤 doing something wrong.

[1] Minute Reprimands: Summary

The [1] Minute Reprimand 🔒 well when 😊:

[1]. Tell 🧍 beforehand that 😊 👉 going to let them know how 🙈 👉 doing and in 😟 uncertain terms, the 🥇 half of the reprimand:

[2]. Reprimand 🧍🧍 immediately.

😊. Tell 🧍 😊 🙈 did wrong: be specific.

[4]. Tell 🧍 how 😊 feel about 😊 🙈 did wrong: and in 😟 uncertain terms.

[5]. ✋ for a few 🥇 of uncomfortable 🔇 to let them feel how 😊 feel.

The 🥇 half of the reprimand:

[6]. 🤝, or touch them in a [1] that lets them know 😊 👉 honestly ↔ their side.

[7]. Remind them how much 😊 value them.

[8]. Reaffirm that 😊 😊 well of them but not of their performance in this situation.

[9]. Realize that when the reprimand is over, it's over.

The young 😊 may not 📖 believed in the effectiveness of the 1️⃣ Minute Reprimand if 🧑 hadn't personally experienced its effect. There was 😊 🔨 that 🧑 felt uncomfortable. And 🧑 did not want to experience it again.

However, 🧑 knew that everyone made mistakes now and then, and that 🧑 might very well receive another reprimand some day. But 🧑 knew if it came from the 1️⃣ Minute 👤, that it would be fair; that it would be a comment ↔ 🔨 behavior and not ↔ 🔨 worth as a 🧑.

As 🧑 headed toward the 1️⃣ Minute Manager's 🏢, 🧑 kept 🙂 about the simplicity of 1️⃣ Minute Management.

All 3️⃣ of the 😊 made sense — 1️⃣ Minute Goals, 1️⃣ Minute Praisings, and 1️⃣ Minute Reprimands. "But why do 👥 👥"? 🧑 wondered. "Why is the 1️⃣ Minute 👤 the most productive 👤 in the company"?

The 1 Minute Manager Explains

WHEN he got to the 1 Minute Manager's, secretary said, "you can go right in. He's been wondering when you'd be free to see him".

As the young man entered the office, he noticed again how clear and uncluttered it was. He was greeted by a warm smile from the 1 Minute Manager.

"Well, did you find out why I call myself a 1 Minute Manager. I set 1 Minute Goals with your people to make sure they know what they're being held accountable for and what good performance looks like.

I then try to catch them doing something right so I can give them a 1 Minute Praising. And then, finally, if they have all the ability to do something right and they don't, I give them a 1 Minute Reprimand".

"What do you think about all that"? asked the 1 Minute Manager.

"I'm amazed at how simple it is", said the young 👤, "and yet it 📱: 😊 🌐 results. I'm convinced that it certainly 📱 for 😊".

"And it will for 😊 too, if you're willing to do it", the 🐿 insisted.

"Perhaps", said the young 👤, "but 😊 would be ✚ likely to do it if 😊 could understand ✚ about why it 📱"

"That's true of everyone, young 👤. The ✚ 😊 understand why it 📱, the ✚ apt 😊 👈 to use it. I'd be 😊, therefore, to tell 😊 😨 😊 know. Where do 😊 want to 🆕"?

"Well, 🕯 of all, when 😊 💬 about 1️⃣ Minute Management, do 😊 really 😌 it takes a minute to do all the kinds of 🍗 😊 need to do as a 🐿"?

"😵, not always. It just is a 🔽 to say that 🅱 a 🐿 is not as complicated as 👫 would 📷 😊 believe. And also managing 👫 doesn't take as long as you'd 😏. 🆘 when 😊 say 1️⃣ Minute Management, it might take ✚ than a minute for each of the 🔑

elements 😊 goal setting, but it's just a symbolic term. And very often it does take only a minute.

"Let me 💻 😊 1️⃣ of the 📕 😊 keep 🔛 my desk".

When 🧑 looked, the young 😊 saw:

The Best
Minute

😊 Spend

Is The 1️⃣

😊 Invest

In 👫

"It's ironic", the 🧑 said. "Most companies spend 50% to 70% of their 😊 🔛 people's salaries. And yet 👀 spend — than 1️⃣ % of their budget to 🖼 their 👫. Most companies, in fact, spend ➕ ⏱ and 😊 🔛 maintaining their 🏛 and equipment than 👀 do 🔛 maintaining and developing 👫".

"😊 never thought of that", the young 😊 admitted. "But if 👫 🔵 results, then it certainly makes 👍 sense to invest in 👫 ".

"Exactly", the 🧑 said. "😊 🙏 😊 had had someone invest in me sooner when 😊 🥇 went to 🏢 ".

"😊 do 😀 😊"? the young 😠 asked.

"Well, in most of the organizations 😊 worked in before,

😊 often didn't know 😊 😊 was supposed to be doing. 😊

1️⃣ bothered to tell me. If 😊 asked me whether 😊 was

doing a 👍 job, 😊 would say either '😊 don't know' or '😊

😊 SOS'. If 😊 asked why 😊 thought SOS, 😊 would reply, '😊

haven't been chewed out by my boss lately' or '😊 NEW

is 👍 NEW'. It was almost as if my main motivation

was to avoid punishment "

"That's interesting", the young 😠 admitted. "But I'm

not sure 😊 understand it".

Then 👤 added anxiously, "In fact, if it's all 🔗 with

😊, maybe 😊 could understand 🐑 better if 😊 could 🔟

to some of the 'why' ? . Let's NEW with 1️⃣

Minute Goal Setting. Why does it 🐴 SOS well"?

Why [1] Minute Goals [briefcase]

"YOU want to know why [1] Minute Goals [briefcase]", the [manager] said. "Fine". [man] got [up] and began to pace slowly around the room.

"Let me give [you] an analogy that might [help]. I've seen a lot of unmotivated [people] at [work] in the various organizations I've been employed in over the years. But I've never seen an unmotivated [person] after [work]. Everyone seems to be motivated to do something.

"[1] [bowler], for example, [you] was [confused] and [you] saw some of the '[unmotivated] employees' at [work] from my last organization. [1] of the real [unmotivated] [people], who [you] remembered all too well, took the [ball] and approached the [lane] and rolled the [ball]. Then [man] started to [shout] and yell and [jump] around. Why do [you] [think] [man] was [excited] [you]"?

"Because [man] got a strike. [man] had knocked [down] all the pins".

"Exactly. Why don't [you] [think] [man] and other [people] [point] that excited at [work]"?

"Because [man] doesn't know where the pins [are] ", smiled the young [man]. "[you] [got] it. How long would [man] want to [bowl] if there were [no] pins"?

"⸻", said the 🕐 Minute 🐵. "Now 😊 can 👁️
🙂 happens in most organizations. 😊 believe that most
🐵 know 🙂 👥 want their 🔧 to do. 👥
just don't bother to tell their 🔧 in a ⬆️ 👥 would
understand. 👥 assume 👥 should know. 😊 never
assume anything when it comes to goal setting.
When 😊 assume that 🔧 know what's expected of
them, 😊 ⬅️ 🔧 an ineffective form of 😊.
😊 put the pins 🎳 but when the bowler goes to roll the
🎳, 🧍 notices there is a sheet across the pins. 🆘 when
🧍 rolls the 🎳, and it slips under the sheet, 🧍 👂 a
crack but doesn't know how many pins 🧍 knocked 👇.
When 😊 ask him how 🧍 did, 🧍 says, 😊 don't know. But
it felt good."
"It's 😊 🧤 ✌️ at ⛳. A lot of my 💀 🎴
given 🎳 ✌️ and when 😊 asked them why, 👥 said,
'Because the courses ☞ too crowded'. When 😊 suggested
that 👥 🧤 at ⛳, 👥 laughed because who would
ever 🧤 ✌️ without 🅱️ able to 👁️ the pins?
It's the same with 👁️ ⚽. How many 🔧
in this 🎽 would 🦵 in front of their TV's ↔️ a

Sunday ☀ or Monday 🌀 and 👁 🥅 👥

run 💰 and 🏑 the field if there were 🌍 goals to 🍃

at or any 🆙 to 💯"?

"Yeah! Why is that"? asked the young 🐱.

"It's all because clearly the 💯 1️⃣ motivator of

👫 is feedback 🔛 results. In fact, 📚 🖼 another

🆙 🎯 that's worth 🌀: 'Feedback is the

🍩 of Champions'. Feedback keeps us going.

Unfortunately, however, when most 🐿 realize that

feedback 🔛 results is the 💯 1️⃣ motivator of

👫, 📚 usually set 🥉 a 🏅 form of 🍩:

When the bowler goes to the 〰 to roll the 🏀, the pins

☞ still 🥉 and the sheet is in 🏆 but now there is

another ingredient in the 🎱: a supervisor standing

behind the sheet. When the bowler rolls the 🏀, 🧍 🍃

the crash of the 🍁 pins, and the supervisor holds 🥉

🥉 🌀 to signify 😃 knocked 🏑 🥉 pins.

Actually, do most 🐿 say 😃 got 🥉"?

"🌀", the young 🐱 smiled. "📚 usually say 😃

missed 8️⃣"

"[emoji] [emoji]"! said the [1] Minute [emoji]. "The ?
[emoji] always used to ask was why doesn't the [emoji] 'lift
the sheet [emoji]' [emoji] both [emoji] and [emoji] subordinate can [emoji] the
pins. Why? Because [emoji] has the [emoji] [emoji]
tradition 'Performance Review' [emoji] [emoji]".

"Because [emoji] has Performance Review [emoji] [emoji]"?
wondered the young [emoji].

"Right. [emoji] used to call that 'NIHYSOB' which stands for
'Now [emoji] [emoji] [emoji]; [emoji] [emoji]". Such [emoji] don't tell
their [emoji] [emoji] [emoji] expect of them; [emoji] just [emoji]
them alone and then '[emoji]' them when [emoji] don't perforin
at the desired level".

"Why do [emoji] suppose [emoji] would do that"? the young
[emoji] inquired, [B] very familiar with the truth in the
manager's comments.

"[emoji] [emoji] can [emoji] [emoji]", said the [emoji].

"[emoji] do [emoji] [emoji], [emoji] [emoji] can [emoji] [emoji]"? asked the
young [emoji].

"How do [emoji] [emoji] [emoji] would be viewed by your boss if
[emoji] rated everyone that reported to [emoji] at the highest
level [emoji] your performance review [emoji]"?

"As a 'soft touch', as someone who could not discriminate between 👍 performance and poor performance".

"Precisely", said the 🧑. "In 📋 to 👁 👍 as a 🧑 in most organizations, 😊 🖼 to catch some of your 👥 doing 🐘 wrong. 😊 🖼 to 🖼 a few winners, a few 💥, and everyone else somewhere in the middle. 😊 👁, in this 📄 🔍 🖼 a normal distribution-curve mentality. 😊 remember 📖 🧍 when visiting my son's 🎓, 😊 observed a fifth-grade teacher 📖 a 🖼 capitals 💯 to her class. When 😊 asked her why 🧍 didn't put atlases around the room and let the kids use them during the 💯, 🧍 said, '😊 couldn't do that because all the kids would 🟦 💯 🖼'. As though it would be 🖐 for everyone to do well.

"I remember once 🚶 that when someone asked Einstein 😊 🤚 🎵 💯 was, 🧍 went to the 🎵 🍞 to 👁 it 👓".

The young 😃 laughed. "You're kidding".

"😃, I'm not kidding. 🧍 said 🧍 never cluttered 🧠 mind with 🖼 🧍 could 🔍 somewhere else.

"Now, if 😊 didn't know better", the 🧑 continued,

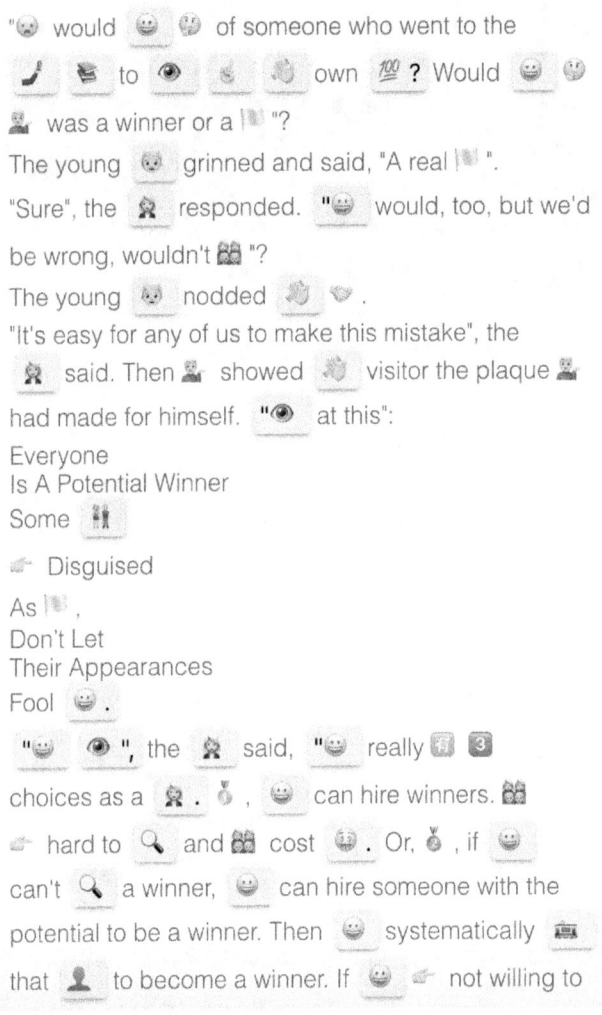

" would of someone who went to the to own 100? Would was a winner or a "?

The young grinned and said, "A real ".

"Sure", the responded. " would, too, but we'd be wrong, wouldn't "?

The young nodded .

"It's easy for any of us to make this mistake", the said. Then showed visitor the plaque had made for himself. " at this":

Everyone
Is A Potential Winner
Some

Disguised

As ,
Don't Let
Their Appearances
Fool .

" ", the said, " really choices as a . , can hire winners. hard to and cost . Or, , if can't a winner, can hire someone with the potential to be a winner. Then systematically that to become a winner. If not willing to

do either of the 💰 🪙 (and 😀 👉 continually amazed at the 💯 of 👤 who won't spend the 💵 to hire a winner or take the ⏱️ to 🖥️ someone to become a winner,) then there is only the 💰 choice 🔜 :
📱 "

That stopped the young 😀 😮 . 👤 put ✋ 💥 📱 and ✏️ and said. "📱 "?

The 👤 laughed quietly. "That's just my attempt at humor, young 😀 . But when 😀 😮 about it, there 👉 many 👤 who 👉 🔗 their 📱 daily: 'I 🛐 this 👤 🏛️ out'. "

"Oh", the young 😀 said seriously. "Well, let's take the 💰 choice. If 😀 hire a winner, it's really easy to be a 📱 Minute 👤 , isn't it"?

"It sure is", said the 👤 with a 😀 . 👤 was amazed at how 😄 the young 😀 was now; as though 🅱️ ➕ 😄 made a 👤 a better 👤 . "All 😀 📱 to do with a winner is do 📱 Minute Goal Setting and let them run with the 🏀 ".

"😀 understand from Ms. 🐿️ , sometimes 😀 don't

even 🐢 to do that with her", said the young 🐭.

"She's absolutely 👍", said the 🐵. "She's

forgotten ➕ than most 👫 know around 📌. But

with everyone, winner or potential winner. 1️⃣ Minute

Goal Setting is a basic 🆑 for productive behavior".

"Is it true that 😊 matter who initiates the 1️⃣ Minute

Goal Setting", the young 🐭 asked, "each goal always

has to be written ✍️ 🔛 a 📄 sheet of 🖨️ "?

"Absolutely", insisted the 1️⃣ Minute 🐵.

"Why is that 🆘 important"?

"So 👫 can review their goals frequently and then

check their performance against those seals".

"I understand 😃 📷 them ✏️ ✍️ only their major

goals and responsibilities and not every aspect of their

job", the young 🐭 said.

"Yes. That's because 😊 don't want this to be a 📄 mill.

😊 don't want a lot of pieces of 📄 filed away

somewhere and looked at only once a year when it's ⌚

for 🔜 year's goal setting or performance review, or

some such 🐘.

"As 😊 probably saw. everyone who 🏢 for me has a

plaque near them that 👁️ 😊 this". 🐵 showed 📸

visitor 🐭 copy of the plaque.

Take A Minute:

👁 At Your Goals

👁 At
Your Performance

👁 If Your Behavior
Matches Your Goals

The young 🐵 was amazed. He'd missed this in 🐾 brief
visit. "😃 never saw this", 🐱 said. "It's terrific. Could 😄 🉐
1️⃣ of these plaques"?

"Sure", the 🐱 said. "I'll arrange it".

As 🐱 was ✏ 🍴 some of 😄 🐱 was 🎓,
the aspiring 🐱 said, without lifting 🍴 🐾 🔔,

"😃 know, it's difficult to 🎓 everything there is to
🎓 about 1️⃣ Minute Management in such a short ⌚.
There's certainly ➕ I'd 😄 to 🎓 about 1️⃣ Minute
Goals, for instance, but maybe 😄 could do that later.

"Could 👥 move to 1️⃣ Minute Praisings now"? asked
the young 🐵, as 🐱 looked 🍴 from 🐾 📕.

"Sure", said the 1️⃣ Minute 🐱 "You're probably
wondering why that 🐜, too".

"😃 certainly 👉 ", the visitor responded.

Why [1] Minute Praisings [img]

LET'S [img] at a few examples", the [1] Minute [img]

said. "Maybe then it will be clear to [img] why [1]

Minute Praisings [img] [img] well".

"I'd [img] that", said the young [img].

"I'll [img] with a pigeon example and then move [img] to

[img] ", said the [img]. "Just remember young [img],

[img] [img] not pigeons. [img] [img] + complicated.

[img] [img] aware, [img] [img] for themselves and [img]

certainly don't want to be manipulated by another [img].

Remember that and respect that. It is a [img] to [img]

management.

"With that in mind, let us [img] at several simple examples

which [img] us that [img] all seek [img] feels [img] to us and

[img] avoid [img] feels [img] to us.

"Suppose [img] [img] an untrained pigeon that [img] want to

[img] a [img] in the lower left-hand corner and run across

the [img] to the upper right-hand corner and push a lever

with [img] [img] foot. Suppose that not too far from the [img]

[img] [img] [img] a pellet [img]; that is, a [img] that

can release pellets of [img] to reward and reinforce the

pigeon. 😮 do 😊 😀 is going to happen if 📖 put the pigeon in the 🖼️ and 🍳 until the pigeon runs over to the upper right-hand corner and pushes the lever with 🤚 👣 foot before 📖 give him any 🐟 "? asked the 1️⃣ Minute 🧑.

"He would starve to 💀 ", responded the young 😊.

"You're 👉. We're going to lose a lot of pigeons. The pigeon is going to starve to 💀 because 🧑 doesn't 📖 any 👇 😊 🧑 is supposed to do.

"Now it's actually not too hard to 🎬 a pigeon to do this task. All 😊 📖 to do is to 🐦 a 〰️ not too far from where the pigeon 🔄 the 🖼️. If the pigeon 🔁 the 🖼️ and crosses the 〰️ — bang — the pellet 🍚 goes off and the pigeon 🔘 fed. Pretty 🔜 😊 📖 the pigeon 🏃 to that spot, but 😊 don't want the pigeon there. Where do 😊 want the pigeon"?

"In the upper right-hand corner of the 🖼️ ", said the young 😊.

" 👉 "! the 1️⃣ Minute 🧑 confirmed. "Therefore, after a while 😊 👆 rewarding the pigeon for 🏃 to that spot and 🐦 another 〰️ which isn't too far from the last 〰, but is in the 🔙 of the goal; the upper right-hand corner of the 🖼. Now the pigeon 🆕 🐾 around 💥 😋 spot and doesn't 🉐 fed. Pretty 🔜 though, the pigeon makes it across the 🆕 〰 and — bang — the 👑 goes off again and the pigeon 🉐 fed.

"Then 😊 🍴 another 〰. Again this 〰 has to be in the 🔙 of the goal, but not too far away that the pigeon can't make it again. 👬 keep setting 🔙 these 〰 closer and closer to the upper right-hand corner of the 🖼 until 👬 won't feed the pigeon unless 🚶 🔼 the lever and then finally only when 🚶 🔼 the lever with 🐾 🔜 foot".

"Why do 😊 set 🔙 all these little goals?" wondered the young 🐷.

"By setting 🔙 these series of 〰, 👬 🔜 establishing goals that the pigeon can achieve. 🆘 the 🔑 to 🐰 someone to do a 🆕 task is, in the beginning, to catch them doing something approximately 🔜 until 👬 can eventually 🍀 to do it exactly 🔜.

"👬 use this concept all the ⌚ with kids and 🐶, but 👬 somehow forget it when 👬 🔜 dealing with big 👫: adults. For example, at some of these 🏃

Aquariums 😊 👁 around the 🗾, 🏢 usually ⬅END the 🖥 by 🏢 a huge 🐋 ⚓ over a rope which is 🆙 🆙 the 💧. When the 🐋 comes 🌱 🧍 drenches the 🍼 ten rows."

"The 👫 🥄 that 🖥 mumbling to themselves. That's unbelievable. How do 🏢 🏦 that 🐋 to do that'?

"Do 😊 😊 🏢 go out in the 🌊 in a 🚤 ", the 🧍 asked, "and put a rope out over the 💧 and yell, '🍬, 🍬 ! ' until a 🐋 ⚓ out of the 💧 over the rope? And then say, 'Hey, let's hire him. He's a real winner'. "

"🙈 ", laughed the young 🐱, "but that really would be 👋 a winner".

The 🍬 😊 enjoyed the 😄 🏢 shared.

"You're ➡ ", the 🧍 said. "When 🏢 captured the 🐋, 🧍 knew 🖥 about ⚓ over ropes. 🆘 when 🏢 began to 📺 him in the large 🎱, where do 😊 😊 🏢 started the rope"?

"At the 🔽 of the 🎱 ", answered the young 🐱.

"Of course"! responded the 🧍. "Every ⌚ the 🐋 swam over the rope — which was every 🔋 🧍 swam past — 🧍 got fed. ➡SOON, 🏢 👋 the rope a little.

"If the 🐋 swam under the rope, 👤 didn't 🍴 fed during 🎪 . Whenever 🐋 swam over the rope, 🐋 got fed. 🆘 after a while the 🐋 started ⬆️ over the rope all of the ⏰ . Then 🔭 started raising the rope a little higher".

"Why do 🔭 raise the rope"? asked the young 👹 .

" 🕐 ", the 👤 began, "because 🔭 were clear 🔛 the goal: to 📷 the 🐋 ↕️ 🆙 out of the 💧 and over the rope.

"And 🕐 ", the 1️⃣ Minute 👤 pointed out. "it's not a very exciting 📺 for a trainer to say, 'Folks, the 🐋 did it again'. Everybody may be 👁 in the 💧 but 🔭 can't 👁 anything. Over a period of ⏰ 🔭 keep 🔛 raising the rope until 🔭 finally 🍴 it to the surface of the 💧 . Now the 🐳 🐋 knows that in 📋 to 🍴 fed, 👤 has to ↕️ partially out of the 💧 and over the rope. As 🔜 as that goal is reached, 🔭 can 🔄 raising the rope higher and higher out of the 💧 ".

"🆘 that's how 🔭 do it", the young 👹 said. "Well, 😊 can understand now how 📺 that method 👥 with 👹 , but isn't it a bit much to use it with 👥 "?

"😊, it's very natural in fact", the 🧎 said. "📖 all
do essentially the same 🐎 with the 👶👶 care
for. How do 😀 😀 😀 📷 them to walk? Can 😀
imagine standing a 👶 🦶 and 🆕 Walk", and when
🧑 🍁 🦶 😀 🔨 him 👋 and spank him and say, '😤
told 😀 to walk'. 😊, 😀 stand the 👶 🦶 and the 🥇
day 🧑 wobbles a little bit, and 😀 😋 all excited and
say, '🧑 stood, 🧑 stood', and 😀 😰 and 🥰 the 👶.
The 🔢 day 🧑 stands for a moment and maybe wobbles
a 🦵 and 😀 🏃 all over him with kisses and 😘.
"Finally the 👶, realizing that this is a pretty 👍 deal,
🆕 to wobble 🦵 legs ➕ and ➕ until 🧑
eventually walks.
"The same 🐎 goes for 📷 a 👶 to speak.
Suppose 😀 wanted a 👶 to say, 'Give me a 🥛 of
💧, 🙏'. If 😀 waited until the 👶 said the whole
sentence before 😀 gave her any 💧, the 👶 would
🐌 of thirst. 🆘 😀 🆕 off by 🆕 '💧, 💧'. All
of a sudden 1️⃣ day the 👶 says, 'Waller'. 😀 ❗ all
over the 🏆, 😀 and 😰 the 👶, 🥰 grandmother ↔️
the 🤙 🆘 the 👶 can say 'Waller, waller". That
wasn't '💧', but it was close.

"Now 😊 don't want a kid going into a 🏪 at the age of twenty-one asking for a 🍺 of 'waller' 🆘 after a while 😊 only 👍 the 🆔 '💧' and then 😊 begin 🔀 '🙏'.

"These examples illustrate that the most important 🐘 in 👶 somebody to become a winner is to catch them doing something 👉: in the beginning approximately 👉 and gradually 📦 them towards the desired behavior. With a winner 😊 don't 🏠 to catch them doing 🐘 👉 very often, because 👍 performers catch themselves doing 🐘 👉 and 👉 able to be self-reinforcing".

"Is that why 😊 observe 🆕 👫 a lot in the beginning", asked the young 👶, "or when your ➕ experienced 👫 👉 🌟 a 🆕 project"?

"👍", the 1️⃣ Minute 🐵 said. "Most 🐵 🍖 until their 👫 do something exactly 👉 before 🎁 👏 them. As a result, many 👫 never 🕐 to become 🆙 performers because their 🐵 concentrate 🔀 catching them doing 🐘 wrong: that is, anything that 🌸 short of the final desired performance. In our pigeon example, it would be 😊

putting the pigeon in the 📖 and not only 🐦 until 🧍

🔘 the lever to give him any 🍴 but putting some

electric grills around the 📖 to punish him periodically

just to keep him motivated".

"That doesn't 👀 😊 it would be very effective", the

young 💀 suggested.

"Well, it isn't", agreed the 1️⃣ Minute 🧍. "After

🔵 punished for a while and not knowing 😊

acceptable behavior is (that is, 🔘 the lever,) the

pigeon would go into the corner of the 📖 and not move.

To the pigeon it is a hostile 🔺 and not worth

taking any risks in.

"That is 😊 👥 often do with 🆕 , inexperienced

🧍‍♂️ . 👥 welcome them aboard, take them around to

meet everybody, and then 👥 ✂️ them alone. Not only

do 👥 not catch them doing anything approximately ✍️ ,

but periodically 👥 ⚡ them just to keep them 📦 .

This is the most popular leadership 🏆 of all. 👥 call it

the '✂️ alone-zap' 🏆 . 😊 ✂️ a 👤 alone,

expecting 👍 performance from them, and when 😊

don't 🔵 it, 😊 ⚡ them".

"😊 happens to these 👥 "? asked the young 💀 .

"If you've been in any organization, and 😊 understand

you've visited several", the 👨‍💼 said, "😀 know,
because you've seen them. 👥 do as little as possible.
And that's what's wrong with most businesses today.
Their 👫 really do not produce either quantity or
quality. And much of the reason for this poor 👨‍💼
performance is simply because the 👫 ☞ managed 🆘
poorly".
The young 🐱 put 💅 📘 ✒ . 🧑 thought about
🐱 🧑 just heard. 🧑 was beginning to 👁 1️⃣ Minute
Management for 🐱 it is: a practical 👨‍💼 🔧 .
It was amazing to him how well something as simple as
the 1️⃣ Minute 🐚 worked: whether it was inside
or outside the 👨‍💼 🌐 .
"That reminds me of some 🐒 of mine", the young
🐱 said. "👥 called me and said that they'd gotten a
🆕 🐒 . 👥 asked me 🐱 😀 thought of their planned
method of 🐶 the 🐒 ".
The 👨‍💼 was almost afraid to ask, "How were 👥
going to do it"?
"👥 said if the 🐒 had an accident 🔛 the rug, 👥
were going to take the 🐒 , shove 🖐 👇 in it, 📷
him 🔛 the butt with a 🔨 and then throw the 🐒
out this little window in the 🏠 into the ⬅ yard —

where the 💀 was supposed to do 🧹 job.

Then, 📖 asked me 😊 😄 thought would happen with this method. 😊 laughed because 😊 knew 😊 would happen. After about 3️⃣ days the 💀 would 🔺 ↔️ the 😊 and ❗ out the window. The 💀 didn't know 😊 to do, but 👤 knew 👤 had better clear the area".

The 🐵 roared 🧹 approval.

"That's a 🏴 story", 👤 said. "😊 👁️, that's 😊 punishment does when 😊 use it with somebody who lacks confidence or is insecure because of lack of experience. If inexperienced 👥 don't perform (that is, do 😊 😄 want them to do,) then rather than punish them 📖 need to go 🔙 to 1️⃣ Minute Goal Setting and make sure 📖 understand 😊 is expected of them, and that 📖 📗 seen 😊 🧹 performance 👁️ 😊".

"Well, then, after 😊 📗 done 1️⃣ Minute Goal Setting again", the young 😊 asked, "do 😊 try to catch them doing something approximately 🧹 again"?

"Precisely 🆘", the 1️⃣ Minute 🐵 agreed. "You're always 📹 to 🔨 situations in the beginning where 😊 can give a 1️⃣ Minute 🍯". Then, 👁️ the young 😊 straight in the 👀, the 🐵 said, "😊

👉 a very enthusiastic and receptive learner. That makes me feel 👍 about sharing the 🌐 of 1️⃣ Minute Management with 😊". 👥 both smiled. 👥 knew a 1️⃣ Minute 🐢 when 👥 heard 1️⃣.

"😊 sure enjoy a 🖐️ ➕ than a reprimand", the young 😊 laughed.

"😊 😊 😊 understand now why 1️⃣ Minute Goals and 1️⃣ Minute Praisings 🐿️. 👥 really do make 💧 sense to me".

"🦌", said the 1️⃣ Minute 🙇.

"But 😊 can't imagine why the 1️⃣ Minute Reprimand 🐿️", the young 😊 wondered out loud.

"Let me tell 😊 a few 🐘 about it", said the 1️⃣ Minute 🙇.

Why 1️⃣ Minute Reprimands 📷

"THERE ☞ several reasons why the 1️⃣ Minute Reprimand 📷 🆘 well.

"To begin with", the 👤 explained, "the feedback in the 1️⃣ Minute Reprimand is immediate. That is, 😃 🉐 to the individual as 🔜 as 😃 observe the 'misbehavior' or your 📇 💩 system tips 😃 off. It is not appropriate to gunnysack or 💾 💰 negative feelings about someone's poor performance.

"The fact that the feedback is 🆘 immediate is an important lesson in why the 1️⃣ Minute Reprimand 📷 🆘 well. Unless discipline occurs as close to the misbehavior as possible, it tends not to be as helpful in influencing 🐄 behavior. Most 👤 ☞

'gunnysack' discipliners. That is, 👓 store 💰 observations of poor behavior and then some day when performance review comes or 👓 ☞ 😦 in general because the 'sack is 🆘 満 ', 👓 charge in and 'dump everything 🔛 the table'. 👓 tell 👫 all the 🐘

👓 📓 done wrong for the last few weeks or 📅 or more."

The young 😺 breathed a deep sigh and said, "🆘 true".

"And then", the 1️⃣ Minute 👤 went 🔛 , "the

🐒 and subordinate usually ⏎ 👤 yelling at each other about the facts or simply keeping 📖 and resenting each other. The 👤 receiving the feedback doesn't really 👁 😊 👤 or 🙇 has done wrong. This is a version of the 🐑 alone-zap' form of discipline that I've spoken about earlier".

"😊 remember it well", responded the young 😃. "That is certainly something 😊 want to avoid".

"Absolutely", agreed the 🐒. "If 🐒 would only intervene 🕐, 👯 could deal with 1️⃣ behavior at a ⌚ and the 👤 receiving the discipline would not be overwhelmed. 👯 could 👁 the feedback. That's why 😊 😃 performance review is an ongoing process, not something 😊 do only once a year".

"🆘, 1️⃣ reason that the 1️⃣ Minute Reprimand 📷 is that the 👤 receiving the reprimand can ' 👁 ' the feedback, because when the 🐒 deals with 1️⃣ behavior at a ⌚, it seems ✚ fair and clear", the young 😃 summarized.

"👍", the 🐒 said. "And secondly, when 😊 give a 1️⃣ Minute Reprimand, 😊 never 🔻 a person's worth or value as a 👤. Since their OK-ness as a 👤 is not '👐 for grabs', 👥 don't feel 👥 🎴 to defend themselves. 😊 reprimand the behavior only. Thus, my feedback and their own reaction to it is about the specific behavior and not their feelings about themselves as 👤 🎏 .

"🆘 often, when disciplining 👫 , 😠 persecute the individual. My purpose in a 🎴 Minute Reprimand is to eliminate the behavior and keep the 👤".

"🆘 that's why 😊 make the 🥇 half of the reprimand a 🎾 ", the young 🐻 said. "Their behavior is not 👐 . 👥 ☞ 👐 ".

"☝ ", agreed the 🎴 Minute 😠 .

"Why wouldn't 😊 give the 🎾 🥇 and then the reprimand"? suggested the young 🐻 .

"For some reason, it just doesn't 👜 ", insisted the 😠 . "Some 👫 , now that 😊 😴 of it, say that 😊 ☞ Nice 'n' Tough as a 😠 . But to be ✚ accurate, I'm really Tough 'n' Nice".

"Tough 'n' Nice", echoed the young 🐻 .

"☝ ", insisted the 🎴 Minute 😠 . "This is an 😊 philosophy that has worked well for literally thousands of years.

"There is, in fact, a story in 📚 🌍 that illustrates this. Once upon a ⏳, an emperor appointed a 👤 in command. 👤 called this 2️⃣ minister in and, in effect, said to him, Why don't 👥 📋 ✂️ the tasks? Why don't 🙂 do all the punishing and I'll do all the rewarding? The 2️⃣ minister said, Fine. I'll do all the punishing and 🙂 do all the rewarding".

"🙂 😊 I'm going to 🙂 this story", the young 🙂 said. "🙂 will, 🙂 will", the 1️⃣ Minute 👤 replied with a knowing 🙂.

"Now this emperor", the 👤 continued, "→SOON noticed that whenever 👤 asked someone to do something, 👥 might do it or 👥 might not do it. However, when the 2️⃣ minister spoke, 👫 moved. 🆘 the emperor called the 2️⃣ minister 🔙 in and said, Why don't 👥 📋 the tasks again? 🙂 👤 been doing all the punishing ✈️ for quite a while. Now let me do the punishing and 🙂 do the rewarding. 🆘 the 2️⃣ minister and the emperor switched roles again. And, within a 📅 the 2️⃣ minister was emperor. The emperor had been a nice 👤, rewarding and 🅱️ kind to everyone; then 👤 started to punish 👫. 👫

87

said, What's wrong with that codger? and threw him out . When came to for a replacement, said. know who's really to come around now? The 2 minister. , put him into ".

"Is that a true story"? the young asked.

"Who cares"? said the 1 Minute , .

"Seriously", added, " do know this. If tough the behavior, and then supportive of the , it ".

"Do any modern-day examples of where the 1 Minute Reprimand has worked other than in management"? the young asked the wise .

" certainly", the said, "Let me mention : 1 with severe adult behavior and another in disciplining ".

" do when say 'severe adult behavior "?' the young asked.

"I'm about alcoholics in particular", the answered. "About thirty years ago an observant clergyman discovered a technique which is now called 'crisis intervention'. made the discovery when was

[📟] a physician's wife. [👩] was in a Minnesota
[🚑] in critical condition and slowly dying from
cirrhosis of the liver. But [👩] was still [❌] that [👩]
had a [🍺] [⚠️] . When all her family had gathered
at her bedside, the clergyman asked each of them to
describe specific [🍺] incidents [👨‍👩‍👧] had observed.

That's an important part of the [1️⃣] Minute Reprimand.
Before [👤] a reprimand [😊] [📖] to [👁️] the behavior
yourself: [😊] can't depend [🔀] [😊] someone else saw.
[😊] never give a reprimand based [🔀] 'hearsay'. "

"Interesting", the young [💀] broke in.
"Let me finish. After the family described specific
behaviors, the clergyman asked each of the family
members to tell the [😊] how [👨‍👩‍👧] felt about those
incidents. Gathered closely around her, [1️⃣] by [1️⃣] [👨‍👩‍👧]
told her [🍷] [😊] [👩] did, and [🍷] , how [👨‍👩‍👧] felt
about it. [👨‍👩‍👧] were [😊] , [😊] , [😊] . And
then [👨‍👩‍👧] told her how much [👨‍👩‍👧] loved her, and [👨‍👩‍👧]
instinctively touched her and gently said how [👨‍👩‍👧] wanted
her to live and to enjoy life once again. That was why
[👨‍👩‍👧] were [📟] [😖] with her".

"That [❓] [📟] simple", said the young [🐰] , "especially
with something as complicated as a [🍺] [⚠️] .
Did it [📣] "?

"Amazingly [SOS]", the [1] Minute [manager] insisted. "And now there [are] crisis intervention centers all over the [world]. It's not as simple as I've summarized it, of course. But these [3] basic ingredients; telling [people] [they] did wrong; telling [people] how [you] feel about it; and reminding [people] that [they] [are] valuable and worthwhile; lead to significant improvements in people's behavior".

"That's [nothing] short of incredible", the young [man] said.

"[I] know it is", the [manager] agreed.

"[You] said you'd give me [other] examples of how other [people] successfully use methods [like] the [1] Minute Reprimand", the young [man] said.

"[I will], of course. In the [early] 1970's, a family psychiatrist in California also made the same amazing discovery with [families]. [He] had [learned] a lot about bonding — the emotional ties [people] [have] to [people]. [He] knew [what] [people] needed.

[People] need to be in contact with [people] who care about them, to be accepted as valuable just because [they] [are] [people].

"The [psychiatrist] also knew that [people] need to [have] a [spade] called a [spade] — to be pulled up short by [people] who care when 👥 ☞ not behaving well".

"How does that translate", the young 😟 wanted to know, "into practical action"?

"Each 👨‍👩‍👧 is taught to physically touch their 👶 by putting their 🙌 ↔ the child's shoulder, touching 💪 , or if 👤 is young actually 👇 the 👶 in their lap.

Then the 👨‍👩‍👧 tells the 😟 exactly 😊 👤 did wrong and how the 👨‍👩‍👧 feels about it; and in 😟 uncertain terms. (😊 can 👁 that this is very 😊 😟 the family members did for the 😟 😟). Finally, the 👨‍👩‍👧 takes a deep breath, and allows for a few ⏱ of 🤫 , 🆘 the 😟 can feel whatever the 👨‍👩‍👧 is feeling. Then the 👨‍👩‍👧 tells the youngster how valuable and important the 😟 is to the 👨‍👩‍👧 .

"😊 👁 , it is very important when 😊 ☞ managing 👥 to remember that behavior and worth ☞ not the same 🐘 . 😟 is really worthwhile is the 👤 managing their own behavior. This is as true of each of us as 🧑 as it is of each of the 👥 👥 ☞ managing.

"In fact, if 😊 know this", the 🧑 said, as 👤 pointed to 1️⃣ of 🤫 🔧 plaques, "😊 will know the 🔑 to a really successful reprimand.

👀 ☞ Not
Just
Our Behavior

👀 ☞

The 🧍

Managing
Our Behavior

"If 😊 realize that 😊 ☞ managing 👫, and not just their recent behavior", the 🧔 concluded, "😊 will do well".

"It 💡 😊 there's a lot of ⭐ and respect behind such a reprimand", the young 😊 said.

"I'm 😆 😊 noticed that, young 🐭. 😊 will be successful with the 1️⃣ Minute Reprimand when 😊 really care about the welfare of the 🧍 😊 ☞ reprimanding".

"That reminds me", the young 😊 injected, "Mr. Levy told me that 😊 pat him ↔ the shoulder, or 🤝 🙂, or in some other ➕ make contact with him during a 👏. And now 😊 notice that the 👥 ☞ encouraged to touch their 👀 during the scolding. Is touching an important part of the 1️⃣ Minute Praisings and Reprimands"?

"👍 and 😕", the 🧔 answered with a 😊. "👍, if 😊 know the 🧍 well and ☞ clearly interested in [emoji: SOS] the [emoji] to succeed in [emoji] or her [emoji]. And [emoji],

if [emoji] or the other [emoji] has any [emoji] about that.

"Touch is a very powerful [emoji]". the [emoji] pointed

out. "[emoji] [emoji] [emoji] feelings about [emoji: B] touched,

and that needs to be respected. Would [emoji], for instance,

[emoji] someone whose motives [emoji] weren't sure of, to touch

[emoji] during a [emoji] or a reprimand"?

"[emoji]", the young [emoji] answered clearly. "[emoji] really

wouldn't"!

"[emoji] [emoji] [emoji] [emoji] [emoji]", the [emoji] explained. "Touch is

very honest. [emoji] know immediately when [emoji] touch

them whether [emoji] care about them, or whether [emoji] [emoji]

just [emoji] to [emoji] a [emoji] [emoji] to manipulate them.

There is a very simple [emoji] about touching", the [emoji]

continued. "When [emoji] touch, don't take. Touch the

[emoji] [emoji] manage only when [emoji] [emoji] [emoji] them

something: reassurance, [emoji], encouragement,

whatever".

"[emoji: SOS] [emoji] should refrain from touching someone", the

young [emoji] said, "until [emoji] know them and [emoji] know

[emoji] [emoji] interested in their [emoji] : that [emoji] [emoji] clearly

[emoji: ON] their side. [emoji] can [emoji] that.

"But", the young 👤 said hesitantly, "while the 1️⃣ Minute Praisings and the 1️⃣ Minute Reprimands 👁 simple enough, aren't 📖 really just powerful 🔋 for 😊 to 🏢 👫 to do 😊 😊 want them to do? And isn't that manipulative"?

"😆 ☞ ☞ about 1️⃣ Minute Management 🅱 a powerful 🔋 to 🏢 👫 to do 😊 😊 want them to do", the 🧍 confirmed.

"However manipulation is 🏢 👫 to do something 📖 ☞ either not aware of or don't 👍 to. That is why it is 🆘 important to let each 👤 know 👈 front 😊 😊 ☞ doing and why.

"It's 😊 anything else in life", the 🧍 explained. "There ☞ 🐘 that 📷, and 🐘 that don't 📷. 🅱 honest with 👫 eventually 📷. 🔛 the other 🐾, as 😊 🏢 probably learned in your own life, 🅱 dishonest eventually leads to 🌋 with 👫. It's just that simple "

"😊 can 👁 now", the young 👤 said, "where the 🔋 of your management 🎮 comes from: 😊 care about 👫".

"👍", the 🧍 said simply, "😊 guess 😊 do".

The young 😺 remembered how gruff 🐭 thought this special 🐒 was when 🐭 👒 met him.

It was as though the 🐒 could 🚗 👺 mind.

"Sometimes", the 1️⃣ Minute 🐒 said, "😊 🔲 to care enough to be tough. And 😊 ☞, 😊 ☞ very tough ⏫ the poor performance — but only ⏫ the performance. 😊 ☞ never tough ⏫ the 👤".

The young 😺 liked the 1️⃣ Minute 🐒. 🐭 knew now why 👫 liked to 🏠 with him.

"Maybe 😊 would 🔍 this interesting, 👺", the younger 😺 said, as 🐒 pointed to 🎇 📗. "It is a plaque I've created to remind me of how goals — the 1️⃣ Minute Goals — and consequences — the Praisings and the Reprimands — affect people's behavior"

Goals
Begin
Behaviors
Consequences
Maintain
Behaviors

"That's very 🥄"! the 🐒 exclaimed.

"Do 😊 😺 🆘"? the young 😺 asked, wanting to 👂 the compliment once again.

"Young 😺", the 🐒 said very slowly for

emphasis, "it is not my role in life to be a 👤 🌵

recorder. 🙂 do not 📖 ⌚ to continually 🔁 myself".

Just when 🧔 thought 🧔 would be praised, the young 🐱

felt 🧔 was in for another 1️⃣ Minute Reprimand,

something 🧔 wanted to avoid.

The bright young 🐱 kept a straight 🙂 and said

simply, "🐱 "?

👀 looked at each other only for a moment and then

👀 both burst into laughter.

"😄 🙂 🙂, young 🐱 ", the 🧔 said. "How would

🙂 🙂 to go to 💼 📌 "?

The young 🐱 put ✋ 🖐 📕 and stared in

amazement. "🙂 😗 go to 💼 for 🙂 "? 🧔 asked

enthusiastically.

"😗. 🙂 😗 go to 💼 for yourself 🙂 the other 👥

in my department. Nobody ever really 💼 for anybody

else. 🙂 just 🆘 👥 💼 better and in the process 👀

benefit our organization ."

This was, of course, 😗 the young 🐱 had been

👁 for all along.

"I'd 🙂 to 💼 📌 ", 🧔 said.

And 🆘 🧔 did — for some 🧑.

The 🕐 the special 👥 had invested in him paid off. Because eventually, the inevitable happened. 🧑

became a

1 Minute

👥 .

🧑 became a 1 Minute 👥 not because 🧑

thought 😀 1 , or talked 😀 1 , but because 🧑

behaved 😀 1 .

🧑 set 1 Minute Goals.

🧑 gave 1 Minute Praisings.

🧑 gave 1 Minute Reprimands.

🧑 asked brief, important ? ; spoke the simple truth; laughed, worked, and enjoyed.

And, perhaps most important of all, 🧑 encouraged the

👫 🧑 worked with to do the same.

🧑 had even created a pocket size "🎱 Plan" to make it

easier for the 👫 around him to become 1 Minute

👥 . 🧑 had given it as a useful 🎁 to each 👤

who reported to him.

A 🎁 To Yourself

MANY years later, the 👵 looked 🔙 ↔ the ⌚

when 👩 💰 heard of the principles of 1️⃣ Minute

Management. It seemed 😊 a long ⏳ ago. 👩 was 😊

👩 had written 📝 😊 👩 learned from the 1️⃣

Minute 🐵.

👩 had put 🍯 📘 into a 📚, and had given copies to

many 👬.

👩 remembered Ms. Gomez's 📱 to say, "😊 can't

thank 😊 enough. It's made a big difference in my

🏠" That pleased him.

As 👩 thought 🔙 ↔ the past, 👩 smiled. 👩

remembered how much 👩 had learned from the original

1️⃣ Minute 🐵, and 👩 was grateful.

The 🆕 🐵 was also 😊 that 👩 could take the

📖 1️⃣ 🚶 further. By 📤 copies to many

other 👬 in the organization, 👩 had solved several

practical ⚠️.

Everyone who worked with him felt secure. 😨 1️⃣ felt

manipulated or threatened because everyone knew "😶

front" 😊 👩 was doing and why.

[👀] could also [👁] why the seemingly simple [1] Minute Management techniques — Goals, [👏] and Reprimands -- worked [SOS] well with [🧍🧍].

Every [👤] who had their own copy of the [📖] could [📖] and re-read it at their own pace until [👀] could understand it and put it to [👍] use themselves. The [👤] knew [🈵] well the very practical advantage of repetition in [🎓] anything [NEW].

Sharing the [📙] in this simple and honest [⬇] had, of course, saved him a [👍] deal of [⌚]. And it had certainly made [👤] job easier.

Many of the [🧍🧍] reporting to him had become [1] Minute [👤] themselves. And [👀], in turn, had done the same for many of the [🧍🧍] who reported to them. The entire organization had become + effective.

As [👤] sat at [👤] desk [☺], the [NEW] [1] Minute [👤] realized [☺] a fortunate individual [👤] was. [👤] had given himself the [🎁] of [得] greater results in —

[⌚].

:bust: had :clock: to :smile: and to plan: to give :organization_icon: organization the kind of SOS it needed.

:bust: had :clock: to :smile: and stay :earth: .

:bust: knew :bust: did not experience the daily emotional and physical stress other :people: subjected themselves to.

And :bust: knew that many of the other :people: who worked with him enjoyed the same benefits.

:icon: department had fewer costly personnel turnovers, — personal illness, and — absenteeism. The benefits were significant.

As :bust: looked :icon: , :bust: was :smile: :bust: had not waited to use 1 Minute Management until :bust: thought :bust: could do it just :right: .

After :icon: staff had :icon: about this management system, :bust: had asked each :person: who reported to him if :icon: would :smile: to be managed by a 1 Minute :manager: .

:bust: was amused to :graduate: that there was something that :people: really wanted even + than :graduate: how to become a 1 Minute :manager: themselves. And that was to :icon: 1 for a boss!

Once [he] knew this, it was a lot easier for him to clearly tell [his] staff that [he] wasn't sure that [he] could do it just exactly the [way] [he] was "supposed to".

"I'm not accustomed to telling [people] how [they feel] or how [you] feel about [work]", [he] had said. "And I'm not sure [you] can remember to calm [down] after I've given someone a reprimand and reminded them of how [work feels] as a [person]".

The typical [approval] from [his] associates had caused him to [smile]. "Well, [you] could at least give it a try"!

By simply asking if [his] staff wanted to be managed by a [1] Minute [Manager] and by admitting that [he] may not always be able to do it [right], [he] had accomplished something very important.

The [people] [he] worked with felt that [he] was honestly [on] their side from the very beginning. And that made all the difference.

Then the [new] [1] Minute [Manager] got [up] from [his] desk and began to walk about [his] uncluttered [office]. [He] was deep in thought.

[He] felt [good] about himself: as a [person] and as a [manager].

about had paid off handsomely. had risen in the organization, gaining **+** responsibilities and **+** rewards.

And knew had become an effective , because both organization and the in it had clearly benefited from presence.

A 🎁 To Others

SUDDENLY the intercom buzzed and startled the 👤 .

"Excuse me, 😊 , for interrupting 😊 ", 🧑 heard 👩

secretary say, "but there is a young 👤 📞 the 📞 .

🧑 wants to know if 🧑 can come and 💬 to 😊 about

the 🔽 📋 manage 👥 🐕 ".

The 🆕 1 Minute 🧑 was pleased. 🧑 knew

➕ 👶 were 🔙 the 🧑 🌍 . And 🧑

was 😊 that some of them were as keen to 🎓 about

🧑 management as 🧑 had been.

The manager's department was now 🏃 smoothly.

As 😊 might expect, it was 1 of the best operations of

its kind in the 🌍 . 👥 👥 were productive and

😊 . And 🧑 was 😊 too. It felt 😊 to be in 👩

position.

"Come anytime", 🧑 heard himself telling the caller.

And ➡️ 🧑 found himself 💬 to a bright young

👤 . "I'm 😊 to share my management 😊 with

😊 ", the 🆕 1 Minute 🧑 said, as 🧑 showed

the visitor to 👩 couch. " 😊 will only make 1 request of

😊 ".

"😨 is that", the visitor asked.

Simply" the 🧍 began, "that 😀 ..."

Share It With Others

🅱️

www.ingramcontent.com/pod-product-compliance
Lightning Source LLC
Chambersburg PA
CBHW071227170526
45165CB00003B/1024